The 1920's & 30's weren't depressing

When Living
On A Farm

An Appalachian Memoir

LOTUS B. PLOTT

RED PRESS CO., INC.

REDPRESSCO.COM

Published by
Red Press Co., Inc.
http://redpressco.com

Contact Red Press for permissions.
Any recognizable brand or brand name belongs to
the trademarked or copyright owner. No infringement is
intended or ownership implied. Character similarity to
a person, living or dead, is purely coincidental.

Cover Photo of *Otto The Rooster* by Michal Grosicki

Library of Congress Control Number:
2017950806

ISBN 978-0-9985899-4-7

Printed in the United States of America

CONTENTS

INTRODUCTION

With encouragement from friends, Kay and Larry Black, I, Lotus Bradley Plott, am writing selected memories from my teenage years, 1926-1945, and some into my adulthood, for others to enjoy. I do not want to put only my face on this. I want you to try to put yourself as though you were born in the 1920's or before. If not you, think of your parents, grandparents, or an aunt or uncle. Please reminisce. And if you have not written down your memories, please do. I wish I had earlier in life.

I will tell it as I remember it while hoping 95% is true. I will not tell it if I don't think it is right. I won't be like the young girl applying for a job as a nanny. The children's father was asking a lot of questions. "Do you smoke?" "No." "Do you get hungry often?" "No, I eat before I get hungry." "Do you cheat on your boyfriend?" "No." The father said, "Are you telling me you don't have any vices?" The girl said, "I can only think of one." "For goodness sakes, tell me what it is." The girl replied, "I lie."

To understand my life on the farm, first you need to learn about my roots. Grandfather's parents were Hiram Cyrus Rogers (1828-1910) and his wife, Mary Eleanor (1829-?). Grandmother's parents were James Wilson Teague and his wife Adeline. I am not sure of the birth and death dates, but James Teague fought with Hiram Cyrus Rogers in the Civil War. They were companions. After the Civil War, when they both returned to Fines Creek, North Carolina, the son and daughter of these companions got married, hence my grandparents. My mother's parents were Andrew Thaddeus Rogers (1851-1938) and Sara Jane Teague (1856-1933). My mother, Bessie Rogers Bradley (1895 – 1987) was born in Haywood County, North Carolina.

The large cemetery at Fines Creek Memorial Baptist Church in Haywood County is named "Hiram Rogers Cemetery" for my maternal grandfather who gave the land for the first church and cemetery. When the large Baptist Church was built, the name was changed from Hiram Rogers to Fines Creek Memorial Baptist Church.

My grandmother bore 14 babies at home in Fines Creek between 1875 and 1902. Only 11 lived to be adults reaching an average age of 80.4 years. My grandfather lived to be 87, and Grandmother lived to be 77. They saw their children all together only one time, and that was in 1918, included were 19 grandchildren at that time. The children were together one other time in 1947. However, that was after their parents had passed. I am fortunate to have pictures of both of these events.

In 1909, my grandparents with five of their children moved in wagons from Haywood County to Macon County. By that time, the others had grown and were scattered over the country. They camped one night since it was impossible to make the 70-mile trip in one day. Driving it today only takes one and a half hours.

My grandparents had 70 grandchildren born in the years between 1894 and 1932. I have no idea how many greats and great-great grandchildren there are.

My first cousin, Helen Rogers, went to work with the FBI's Ten Most Wanted List when it was first formed. She never married and lived in the same apartment for years near a lot of the Embassies on Wisconsin Avenue, Washington, DC. I visited her several times. One time I visited was after the Cuban Embassy was closed. Looking down from her balcony, we could see the grass was knee high in the Embassy's yard. The Italian Embassy was across the street. Helen was well informed about Washington and world affairs. I felt she was still young when she retired from the FBI.

Helen devoted so much of her life in Europe researching our Rogers history. Thanks, Helen. With the help of Mack Davis, my second cousin and his wife, Juanita, they compiled a book "1000 AD – 2000 AD. A Rogers Family Millennium, from Pirates and Vikings to Kings and Martyrs." I have quoted this book below. (See portrait and photo of Bible.) Several of our former ancestors had noble blood. When children were born out of wedlock, the "Fitz" was added to the names of these children. In the 1400's, Thomas Rogers had the Fitz removed from the Rogers name.

In books listing Martyrs, you will find Rev. John Rogers. He was the first protestant martyr under "Bloody" Mary's reign as queen.

Rev. John Rogers (1505?-1554)

Portrait Taken from H. Hollands "Herwologia Anglica"

English Celebrities of 1620

REV. JOHN ROGERS

Many of SIR JOHN'S descendants served with distinction during the next generations of English history. The best known of these was JOHN ROGERS, the first protestant martyr.

JOHN ROGERS was born in 1507 near Warwick. He attended the College of Cardinals at Oxford and became rector of the Holy Trinity Church in London. About 1534, he went to Antwerp, Belgium as a Catholic priest with a shipping company. While there, he lived at the "English Merchants' House", where he was chaplain. He became friends with a resident, William Tyndale, who was working on a manuscript of a Bible. (See "Bible") He became interested in the Protestant Reformation. Shortly thereafter he renounced Catholicism. In 1536 he married ADRIANA PRATT, and eleven children were born of this marriage.

When Tindale was martyred, Rogers continued his work translating the Bible into English and finished the first complete English edition of the Old and New Testaments to be published (in Antwerp). Since this was a crime punishable by death at the time, it was published under the name of Thomas Matthew, the names of his two favorite apostles.

REV. JOHN ROGERS returned to England in 1548 during the reign of Edward VI, who was sympathetic with the Protestant Reformation, of which Rogers was a leader. In 1553 his family was naturalized by a special act of Parliament. However, during that same year, upon Edward's death, Catholic Mary came to the throne, dedicated to the idea of bringing England back to Catholicism. Rev. Rogers preached a sermon at St. Paul's Cathedral denouncing Queen Mary's religion. He was arrested, brought before a council of church leaders, and given a chance to renounce his faith. This he refused to do; he was taken to Newgate Prison where he remained a year and was never allowed to see his family. On February 4, 1554, he was taken to Smithfield, the "place of the burning" and there gave up his life for his faith. He was "Bloody Mary's first martyr of the Reformation.

1537/1549 Matthew's Bible

35

CHAPTER ONE

Living In The 1920's and 1930's

I know that the 1920's and 30's were the best years to grow up—if you lived on an active, well-run farm with parents who could do anything and taught their children to enjoy working. We also had our church and community families.

We didn't miss what we never had! The Great Depression didn't affect us, since we didn't have much money before, during or after. However, we never considered ourselves to be poor. "Poor" meant skinny and boney, nothing about whether you had money or not. For example, "That poor, skinny cat will die if someone doesn't feed it." There were others who weren't as fortunate as we were to be living so well because they did not live on a farm.

How would you like to live in a community with just two telephones? One was a pay phone in the post office/store and the other one in the postmistress' home. The pay phone was locked up at night. If you needed one for an emergency at night, you would have the wake up the Parrish family. No one wanted to do that! I left home shortly after I turned 17, and we still didn't have a telephone. I am not sure when my parents got one, but I believe it was after daddy died in 1947. The only way you could talk to anyone was in person. We didn't know how to send smoke signals. When we saw people, we were so happy to see them, hug them, and look into their eyes as we talked, smiled, and laughed. I had happiness from within!

How would you like to live on a 170-acre farm and not have an engine or piece of equipment with a motor? My daddy never had a car, a tractor, or lawn mower. He never had boys in the family, just us girls to help him.

How would you like to live in a community without electricity? I am including a contract my father signed with Rabun Land and Water Company to install electricity in our home on May 27, 1940, when I was 14 years old. The price was $28.50 for eight light bulbs hanging in the middle of the room and two light switches. There were no electrical outlets. When my sisters graduated from high school, we still had oil lamps. Of course we knew to get our homework done before dark to avoid using the lamps.

When I was growing up, I never heard the word television, frozen food, credit cards, ball point pens, electric dishwasher (we carried the water up the hill from the spring, built a fire in the cook stove to heat the water, and used two dish pans, one for washing and one for rinsing), washing machine (please read my chapter on washing and ironing clothes), clothes dryer, air conditioner, electric blanket, pantyhose (the women had stockings held up with garters and a seam up the back that had to be kept straight).

We never heard of polio shots, penicillin, or abortion. I never heard of pregnancy or someone going to have a baby. My mother would be away a few hours and come home and say "Dr. Neville brought so and so a little baby boy or a little baby girl." The women in the community always helped Dr. Neville deliver the babies. It seemed it was always at night for mother would be coming home in time to cook breakfast and see us off to school. We never heard of store-bought diapers.

Strange thing, I never heard the words "living together." People got married, then lived together and had babies. When I was growing up, I only knew one person who was divorced. He had remarried and had children older than me so I didn't know what divorce was.

"In the closet" was for clothing, not for coming out. We never heard of fast food, gay rights, electric typewriters, computers, yogurt, men wearing earrings, or ladies wearing pant suits. We thought grass had to be mowed or let the cattle eat it, coke was a cold drink, and pot was used in the kitchen to cook in. There were 5 & 10-cent stores where you could buy things for 5 & 10 cents. "Made in Japan," meant junk.

CONTRACT

Dillard, Georgia, ... *May 27* ...., 19*30*

THIS AGREEMENT, made by and between *Ed Bradley*

hereinafter called the Purchaser and Rabun Land and Water Company.,
hereinafter called the Seller.

WITNESSETH; that for and in consideration of the sum of $...............
the Seller agrees to furnish labor and materials to do certain electric wiring or
other service, as follows:

Install complete *30* ....Ampere capacity *2*....wire Service Entrance. *300*

 , ,, *8*.......lighting outlets in (Res) (Store) (Ch) (Sch) (*1600*

 ,, ,, ...lighting outlets in (garage) (barn) (...............*400*

 ,, ,, *2*....lighting wall switches. *2300*

 ,, ,, ...lighting wall switches, 3 way

 ,, ,, ...convenience outlets, duplex.

Purchaser agrees to pay the Seller for said electric wiring or other service,
as outlined above, the sum of $*2300*........when the wiring or service has
been completed.

All wiring to be in accordance with the National Electric Code. This agreement constitutes the entire contract between the Purchaser and the Seller.

E Hallard Purchaser Signs *Ed Bradley* (Seal)

Witness

Seller
Signs
  RABUN LAND & WATER CO. (Seal)

.... By ....

Witness

CONTRACT

Dillard, Georgia, ... *may 27* ...., 19*40*

THIS AGREEMENT, made by and between *Ed Bradley*
hereinafter called the Purchaser and Rabun Land and Water Company,
hereinafter called the Seller.

WITNESSETH, that for and in consideration of the sum of $ *500*...............
the Seller agrees to furnish labor and materials to build or erect a certain
cut-in or service pole line from transformer or existing secondary line to
provide suitable electric current to Purchaser's residence or place of business,
as follows:

150 Lin. Ft. of No *8* .... two wires @ *3* ....c Per Lin. Ft.

...........Lin. Ft. of No........... three wires @ ....c Per Lin. Ft.

...........Poles........Ft. length, including hardware, @ $ *100* .... each.

...........Pole guys @ $................. each.

TRANSFORMER INSTALLATION

Plan "A"   Under this plan the Purchaser agrees to buy all or adequate
share of transformer installation to provide current for his
residence or place of business *150* and to pay Seller $...............
for transformer installation.

Plan "B"   Under this plan the Purchaser agrees to guarantee the Seller
a minimum monthly revenue of $................. for the first year,
based on existing rates (except as to the minimum monthly bill-
ing) and to deposit with the Seller $................. to cover said
guarantee of revenue, and $................. of said deposit will be
applied to Purchaser's account each month as earned revenue.
In consideration of said guarantee of revenue the Seller will
provide adequate transformer installation at no cost to the Purchaser.

METERS   Meters will be furnished at no cost to Purchaser.

All cut-in or service pole line to be in accordance with National Electric Code.

Purchaser agrees to pay the Seller $................. when the work as outlined
above has been completed

Purchaser agrees to deposit $................. as guarantee of revenue for first
year, in compliance with Plan "B", when transformer capacity has been
provided.

This agreement constitutes the entire contract between Purchaser and Seller.

Purchaser
.... Signs .... (Seal)
Witness
Paid 20 = 5-27-40   Seller
Signs
RABUN LAND & WATER CO. (Seal)

.... By ....
Witness

CHAPTER TWO

Smithbridge Township

My community of Otto was within an area known only as Smithbridge Township until the early 1900's. There is no debate about how Smithbridge Township got its name. The Smith part is easy. Mr. and Mrs. Samuel Smith with a large family came over from Buncombe County, North Carolina, and obtained large tracts of land on the East side of The Little Tennessee River acquired from the State of North Carolina's Treaty with the Cherokee Indians. The bridge part is easy, also. Mr. Smith and his sons built a road and a bridge from the main road across the river to their property. Thereafter the area was known as SMITHBRIDGE TOWNSHIP.

However, there is some debate about where the original bridge was built. The road went through our bottomland on the west side of the Little Tennessee River. I started play-ing on and under a bridge in the 1920's especially when our family was working in the bottomland and we needed to cool off. Our parents let us play at the bridge but not in the water. The river was a dumping ground for dead cattle, horses, chickens, dogs, anything and everything. The bridge was an old bridge then. I could see a foundation of a former bridge that I believe was built in the 1800's.

I have copies of several Warranty Deeds where Mr. Smith sold part of his land. I feel fortunate to have read an Abstract Title where Samuel Smith sold 433 acres 27 March 1839 to Bryant Connelly (now Conley) and where Mr. Connelly sold it to numerous people. This land was along the East side The Little Tennessee River and including some of The Tessentee

Creek where the Tessentee Bottomland Preserve and Rose Stiles' property is now located.

There is another Warranty Deed to George Penland from Samuel Smith. For generations, the Penlands owned a lot of land on the east side of the Little Tennessee River. I believe most of this land was formerly Samuel Smith's property. I know part of it was. During my childhood, the land was owned by Ed and Arie Penland Mozely. I remember the bridge crossing from our land and going between the Mozely's and William and Blanche Parrish's land.

Yes, I believe the original bridge built by the Smith men is the one I could see only the remains of the foundation when I played at the bridge as a child. Or was it a childhood fantasy that I wanted SMITHBRIDGE to originate where I was playing?

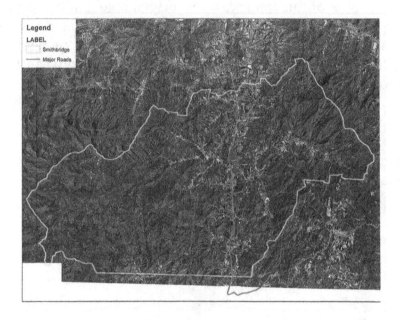

CHAPTER THREE

Origin of Otto, North Carolina

Otto, the community where I was born and raised, was incorporated in 1909; and my grandfather, I. T. Bradley, was appointed mayor. There would not have been a little town of Otto if it had not been for the Tallulah Falls Railroad and my grandparents, and then my father, selling land to people to build other businesses. The Tallulah Falls Railroad bought a 4.91 acres right-of-way and a 0.23 lot to build a depot from my grandparents, I.T. and Elmira Bradley. The survey is dated June 14, 1909, and was recorded at Macon County Court House on July 31, 1909.

All my life I was told about how Otto was named. My grandparents, Isaac Terrell and Elmira Bradley, established a post office in their home for the local folks. They were advised by the U.S. Postal Department they had to have a town name. They were building a room onto their house for the postal boxes when one of the workers didn't show up for work. The next day when he came in to work he said, "I am sorry about yesterday, but my wife had a baby boy." Grandpa asked him, "What did you name him?" He said, "Otto." Grandpa said, "That is what I will submit to the postal department as the town's name." The name was accepted for the new town. My sister, Hazel, was born in 1922. She told me she remembered playing with some of those mail boxes in our grandparents' home before they tore it down.

The correct pronunciation is OT'-TOE. When I go back to Otto and hear the newcomers pronouncing it a different way, it makes me sick. I say, "No, no, it is Ot'-toe." It sounds to me they are saying ah-ta or auto. I can't understand what they are saying.

My grandparents sold most of their farm to my father, Ed Bradley. The sale was recorded in Macon Register of Deeds office on January 7, 1911. I have that deed. A portion of the farm with two buildings on the north side of the branch later went to my Aunt Belle.

All of the original buildings in Otto are now gone. Newer buildings are scattered up and down highway US 441/23 for about ten miles from near the Georgia State line to Union. The highway department took most of the land occupied by Otto when the road was widened several times, so goodbye to the old buildings of Otto. However, the core of the town of Otto still exists, centered on our former land including the community building, fire Department, Asbury Methodist Church, and the former consolidated school.

I have lots of old deeds where my grandparents and my daddy sold land for businesses near the depot site. I remember eight buildings: the post office which was moved to Parrish's store, variety stores, blacksmith shop, restaurant, feed store, and the Depot for passengers and some freight. There was another place to load pulpwood, logs, and crossties.

Coincidentally, my late husband, Donald Plott, had ancestors living in North Carolina, who also had the post office in their home. The postal department advised them they had to have a name of a town. Mr. Plott sent the postal department the names of his three daughters. They chose Maggie, hence Maggie Valley, North Carolina.

Above: A one pound weight used in my family store. It was the first building built and last to be torn down.

The Queen's English

Everyone in the Otto area where I grew up spoke the Queen's English. I was a teenager before I realized I spoke differently from other people out of our area. We never went very far, just to our kinfolk in Haywood County who spoke the same way. Then we went right back home.

Years ago, the Travel and Tourism Division, Department of Commerce of North Carolina, printed a small pocket-sized book, "A Dictionary of the Queen's English." This was so the tourists could understand the people in the Blue Ridge Mountains, Great Smoky Mountains, the Outer Banks of North Carolina, and over into Cocke County, Tennessee. Queen Elizabeth style correspondence has been traced back to such men as Sir Walter Raleigh, Marlowe, Dryden, Bacon, and even William Shakespeare. The little book is divided into three sections:

1. Definitions of English words and phases still used in North Carolina.

2. North Carolina dialect.

3. Expressions you are likely to hear from the original natives.

This is not so much how we sound the word but variations and use of the word. For instance, I always say, "will you hep me?" not, "Will you help me?" The computer is not accepting the word "hep" now. I make the computer show red a lot since I use a lot of words that can't be found in the Webster's Dictionary.

I probably used my way of speaking to my advantage without realizing it. Just before I turned 19 years old, I became a Lumber Wholesaler buying and selling lumber from coast to coast in the USA and Canada. After talking with the men the first time, I never had to tell my name again. They would recognize my voice. Of course it didn't hurt that I was the only woman Wholesaler in the world during my more than 35-year career.

About fifty years ago, The Vancouver morning paper had printed on their front page under "Around Town": "A gal from Kingsport, Tennessee, with a strong southern drawl must have got the wrong number on Monday. She wanted a quote on the price of spruce from Eric Lindsey. Eric told her his Park Board connection didn't mean he could go logging in Stanley Park." (Stanley Park is a beautiful 1000-acre park in the city of Vancouver.) Even though my name was not mentioned, I received a lot of telephone calls and clippings from my lumber manufacturers in Vancouver, British Columbia. They all knew the item was about me.

I still speak the Queen's English and have not tried to change.

"I am plumb wore out with this whole affair."

CHAPTER FIVE

My Mother - Bessie Rogers Bradley

Mother was born September 15, 1895, in Fines Creek, Haywood County, North Carolina. Her family moved to Macon County, North Carolina, in 1909 to the Hickory Knoll Community. Mother married Ed Ray Bradley in January of 1918. Born to them were three girls, Josephine, in May 1919; Hazel, November, 1922; and I arrived April 1926. There were three and a half years between each of us. I didn't know there was Planned Parenthood back then! In March 1943, Rose Hopkins Stiles, then age ten, came to live with us after her mother died.

It was well known that a farm was run or managed like a family enterprise. Each person knew his or her jobs and attended to them. My mother was General Manager and CEO, from planting to harvesting of the garden, cooking, canning, preserving, and storage of food for the winter. In addition, she attended to washing the clothes, ironing, cleaning the house. Also, she was the only one in our family who milked the cow, and that was done twice a day 365 days per year. We had plenty of milk for drinking, making cottage cheese, and making butter, which gave us buttermilk. She made our clothes, too. The list goes on and on.

She was the mother to four daughters, which already sounds like a full job. While we had sheep, before our neighbor's dogs killed all of them, Mother would card the wool, dye the wool, spin the wool into thread, and then knit us stockings, mittens, caps, and sweaters. She would order cloth out of Sears Roebuck's catalogue for seven cents a yard to make our dresses. Sears and Roebuck's catalogue was a big part of our life, not the least part was, when we received a new one, we could take the old one to the outhouse for toilet paper. I do not remember any store-bought toilet paper.

In addition to her duties at home, Mother did so much for Asbury Methodist Church, such as being the treasurer. One thing she disliked was going to members' homes and asking for more money at the end of the church year if the budget was not met - ($1187.00 in 1955-56). Mother also prepared the sacrament for 32 years. I remember very carefully washing and storing the little grape-juice cups until the next time for sacrament.

She was always cooking a special cake or other food and walking miles to take it to our sick neighbors. Our farm surrounded Otto's stores and the post office on three sides. Our friends who walked miles to the stores and post office would stop to rest on our porch and get some good spring water. Mother would insist they stay and eat.

Mother would be in the bed when I went to sleep; but when I was getting up in the morning, she might be coming in the house and would say, "Dr. Neville brought Jane and Joe (or Bill and Betty) a new little baby girl (or boy) last night." We never heard anything about anyone being pregnant. We never heard about the stork or the cabbage head, it was always Dr. Neville. His office was in Dillard, Georgia; but he made house calls all over Smithbridge Township for any sickness or births. My mother was not a midwife, but a lot of the women helped with childbirth, which usually happened at night. That is another reason a lantern was a very important item in our house.

I still have our kitchen table that served as the center of activity in my family's home. The table, now over 100 years old, sat about ten feet from the fireplace, which was our only heat source, except when the cook stove was hot. The table belonged to my daddy's parents before my parents got it when they married in 1918. At this table is where the family ate three meals a day, many times with visitors when an extra leaf made more room for company. Mother used the surface to cut cloth to make our clothes. We gathered around the table to read books and newspapers, play games, or just sit around and talk. The Bible and a lamp stayed on the table, as well as the salt and pepper shakers. Since we cared for our belongings, the table has never been refinished. If this table could only talk, I would love to hear the stories it would tell.

We had a neat, clean house. I remember, after taking the ashes out of the stove and fireplace, we had to dust. We did not have to be reminded. All the ashes had to be saved, for they had many uses on the farm: put in the outhouse to control odors, on bean and potato vines to kill bugs, and was fertilizer for the garden and flowers. In the springtime, we took all the furniture out of a room and scrubbed the floor. We had plenty of splinters after scrubbing the flat grain, yellow-pine floors. We had to be very careful when walking in our bare feet. We left the windows and doors open all day, or maybe two, to dry the floor before moving the furniture back.

During the Depression, there were lots of people walking up and down the highway begging for food. It seemed Mother always had some leftover food even if it was just a piece of cornbread she would give them if they knocked at our door. If no one stopped, she would put the leftovers in a slop bucket for the hogs.

My mother was the best cook in the world. She made the greatest walnut cake. I have tried for years to find someone who made the same kind. I believe the icing was made from walnuts and caramel. Her gingerbread melted in your mouth. No one could make a sweet potato cobbler like my mother. Every time my nephew, Edd Dowdle, visits me, he wants me to make sweet potato cobbler. Mine is not as good as my mother's. My excuse is she had fresh ingredients.

Of course she had fresh milk, butter, buttermilk, streaked meat, ham hocks or any pork that was needed, fresh vegetables right out of the garden, or canned fresh meat, vegetables or fruit. We never worried about calories. In fact, I had never heard that word until I was middle age. After we got utility poles, Mother would say she could go out in the yard and cut my dress pattern out by using the pole, as I was so tall and skinny. Later in life, I learned ladies preferred the word "slender" instead of skinny.

One thing my mother was concerned about was her daughters' postures. She never screamed, "stand up straight"; but she would say, "A dog carries their tail away behind them." When we were seated, she would say, "Remember why God gave you two cushions." She meant, "don't sit on your spine." The last time I saw her hoeing in the garden at age 80, she was standing so straight. She would say "It's not important what you wear as it is how you wear it." She wanted us to take pride in ourselves.

After my father died in 1947, my mother did a good job of keeping up the 154 acres until 1975. We tried to get her to sell some acres and spend the money on herself. She said, "No, I might need it; if not, I will leave it to you girls." Mother and Daddy had already let Otto School and Asbury Methodist Church have most of their highway frontage.

President Roosevelt signed the Social Security Act into law on August 14, 1935. In 1937, it was taken out of workers' paychecks and payments were started in 1941. Farm owners did not have it taken from their employment check, therefore, were not covered by the 1937 Act. In 1954, a law was passed that self-employed farmers were allowed to file taxes for the Social Security if they had net earnings of $400 or more. In 1955, 2.1 million farmers met the minimum income requirements and paid self-employment taxes. That same year, Mother agreed to write down everything, even chickens and eggs she sold. We filed her taxes. In a few months, she called me with anxiety in her voice and said, "When can you come home?" I said, "I don't know, why?" She said, "The government has sent me a welfare check, and I want you to send it back." I thought for a few seconds and realized it was her first Social Security check. I asked her, "How much is the check?" She said, "$26.40, and I want you to send it back." I lived approximately 100 miles from her. I explained I didn't need to come because it was her Social Security check that she had been saving all the figures for the last year so we could file her taxes. It wasn't easy, for most folks did not want to depend on the government for one red cent.

After Mother had several mini strokes, she went to Cleveland, Tennessee to live with my sister, Hazel. In 1976, she had a major stroke. Mother then spent almost 11 years in the Bradley County nursing home. We needed to sell her land to pay all her bills so we could keep her in the same private room for it disturbs patients to change rooms. She had not listened to me about appointing a Durable Power of Attorney. She said, "I am doing all right taking care of myself, and I will continue taking care of myself." The court-appointed attorneys got a big chunk of her money every time we sold a piece of her land. (I beg every person to appoint a Durable Power of Attorney for Financial Decisions and

Health Care. I am up on a stump preaching this.) She did not speak to us for ten years, but I felt she understood a lot of what was going on. She died September 1987 at the age of 92. Thank goodness she paid her own way in the nursing home and did not need the government. If we had had to use some government assistance, she would have died again or come back to haunt us.

Above: Items used in my mother's kitchen.

CHAPTER SIX

My Daddy - Ed Ray Bradley

Daddy's grandparents, Andrew Bradley (1806-1890) and Elizabeth Ray Bradley (1807-1875), had three children; one being my Daddy's father, Isaac Terrell Bradley (1842-1917) married to Nancy Elmina Messer, (1845-1927). When Daddy's grandparents moved from Buncombe County, North Carolina, to Macon County, North Carolina, they had to hide out in a stockade to be protected from the Indians. They saw the Indians putting on war paint. When the Indian fighters arrived, they were watching as the Indians killed some white men. When the Indians left, the white men ran over their dead friends with horses and wagon so the Indians would not come back and get their heads. I wasn't there, so I can't guarantee this, but it is a story I have always heard.

The first Macon County Warranty Deed that I have for Andrew Bradley was for 53 acres they bought in 1838 when he was 32. He kept buying land for years.

Daddy, Ed R. Bradley, (1875-1947) bought 60 acres from G. R. Bradley in December 1905. Then he bought the family home and part of the land from his parents, Isaac Terrell and N. Elmira Bradley, on January 7, 1911. His grandparents, Andrew Bradley and Elizabeth Ray Bradley had previously owned part of it. My daddy kept buying land until he accumulated approximately 170 acres. My parents were married in 1918 during World War I.

My daddy, Ed Bradley, was general manager and CEO of the outside work on our farm. After the highway department took lots of road frontage at different times for widening projects, and the church and the schools were built, 154 acres were left.

FARMERS ARE THE SMARTEST PEOPLE IN ANY BUSINESS OR INDUSTRY. PERIOD. My daddy never had a motor of any kind. He had no car, tractor, lawn mower, or chain saw, etc.. Work was done with brain and brawn. He enjoyed every day of his work and showed it with a look of contentment. But I could never get him to smile in a picture. He always had two working horses, the last ones, I remember were Bill and Jane. He talked horse language to them: gee, haw, whoa, and gitta-up. Together they made the soil "just right" for anything we needed to plant. Daddy enjoyed his horses and working the soil.

Once he bought a Western horse at an auction. He did not know she was expecting. When the foal was born, it was a pinto, white with reddish brown spots; and the spot on its hip looked just like George Washington's head. We had bragging rights on something to "show off". The markings on the foal were a real curiosity.

Daddy managed the crops from season to season and kept the cattle, sheep, hogs, chickens, and ducks doing what they were supposed to do. He kept everything looking neat, such as, fences, barns, and outhouses. He worked winter, spring, summer and fall.

He always had plenty of wood ready for the washing pot, fireplace, and our wood-burning cook stove. He would bring the wood to the back yard with a horse and sled. He would cut and split it into the proper sizes. He would never let me use the axe. My mother, sisters, and I would stack the cut wood up on the back porch and keep a wood box filled by the kitchen stove. The fireplace was the only heat we had. We did burn on one side and freeze on the other.

Daddy taught me that we were in partnership with God. The soil was God's. We did not make it; it was given to us. We saved seeds from year to year (they are now called heirloom seeds) or bought seeds and then planted the seeds. God tended to the sprouting of the plants from the seed. We cultivated the plants so they could absorb the sun, nutrients, and the rain so they could grow. God furnished the sun, nutrients, and the rain. We harvested the crops. We ate food from the crops. The livestock and chickens ate food from the crops. We preserved the harvested food for the winter and thanked God.

From my daddy, I learned how to predict the weather. I don't remember having an actual thermometer on the farm. My father predicted the weather in several ways. One way was by reading the leaves. It was an art of studying. I doubt there is an old timer left who can read the leaves. Yes, it was called "read them" or "read 'em". The favorite way was by watching the mountain laurel leaves. In the winter, every leaf is better than a store-bought thermometer. Leaves stand out like rabbit ears until the weather starts getting cold. Then they droop, partially curl, and fully tighten into a solid roll. Old timers can tell you what the temperature is by how much it has tightened.

What we called laurel is now called rhododendron, which has larger, bolder blooms, which grew in higher elevations such as Roan Mountain and Craggy Garden. Mountain

Laurel had a smaller, more tender and delicate bloom. Rhododendron is now commercially available.

Then there are the old sayings:

*Red sky in the morning is a sailor's warning. Red sky at night is a sailor's delight.

*If leaves on the poplar trees, or their cousins, turn upside down when the wind blows, my daddy would say, "They are showing their bellies, and it will rain in 24 hours."

*If the cattle came in early from the pasture and lay down near the barn, bad weather was approaching.

*Three months after the first katydids begin "hollerin'", the first frost will come.

My daddy always said, "If a snow lingers, it is waiting for another." He was always happy to see a snow cover linger since it would slowly seep into the ground.

The smoke from the chimney told a lot. If smoke goes toward the ground, it will rain soon. If it goes straight up, it will be fair. Different times of the year, the weather can be forecasted by which way the wind is blowing the smoke – east, west, south or north. Other people judge by the moon, wooly worms, when they heard screech and hoot owls, crickets holler, or when butterflies arrived and left. There are so many different ways to read or forecast the weather; I wish I could remember them all. On the farm, we didn't need a meteorologist.

After 90 plus years, I can still hear his telling me, "Don't do it unless you can look back and be proud of it." Both of our parents taught us good work habits and to enjoy working. I did enjoy most of my work; we considered it "doing our part". I was first a water-boy about the age of four or five. This was taking a pail of water from the spring to the fields to my sisters and Daddy. I would go so often Daddy said I was going to drain the bottom of the spring out. He was teasing.

My daddy never had a store-bought toothbrush using homemade black gum twigs as shown in the photo on page twenty-six. He kept one in his shirt pocket all the time for daily use. About once a week, he would mix salt and soda together and scrub his teeth. He said these brushes were the only way to take care of his gums. On my daddy's 61st birthday was the only time he went to the dentist in his whole life. He wouldn't have gone then if not for an abscessed tooth he needed to have pulled. When he died, he had all the rest of his teeth.

Above: Black Gum "toothbrushes" and the plant they come from.

Daddy would not invite anyone into our house who was drinking alcohol. He would say, "Please come back tomorrow when you are not drinking and you are yourself." The word spread, and he didn't have to tell many people.

People were so good to us, and we were good to everyone. For instance, Prince Curtis was out of a milking cow. They lived about four miles from us, over on the other side of our mountain. Daddy said, "Prince, I would be glad to loan you a milking cow until yours is ready to milk again." They took one of our milking cows home with them. The cow and a mule got out of Prince's fence. They found the mule, but not our cow. In a few days, Prince came to our house and said, "Mr. Bradley, I hate to tell you; but I have lost your cow." Daddy laughed and said, "No, Prince. She came home last night." They were astonished and never figured it out. Did she come through the woods to the other side of the mountain, or did she come down the road?

In his whole life, my daddy did not go into debt one penny for anything. If he did not have the money or something he could swap, he did not buy. I wish I had followed his wisdom. He also knew the difference between Want and Need.

He never disciplined his girls. He left that to our mother. All of us girls would be wrestling with him on the floor. When he got tired of it, he would say, "We need to quit." If we didn't, he would say, "Stop, or I am going to call your mother." We stopped.

My daddy was also generous. Most of the children of the community lived on the Otto side and highway side. Many days in the winter and early spring, the children could not get to school due to flooding of the Little Tennessee River that went through our bottomland. For years, Daddy tried to get a consolidated school built along the highway on our property and joining Otto. When the old school burned, the county decided to build. For only $275, in 1932, Daddy sold them two and three-quarters acres to build a two-room school. In April 1940, for $500, the county bought more land for the consolidated school. Then the WPA workers built the school. My parents let Asbury Methodist Church and the county (for the building of two schools) have most of our road frontage, and more good, tillable land, all on one side of the highway.

My parents were contented and lived a good life.

CHAPTER SEVEN

Early Basic Lessons

Our first education that lasts for an entire life was before we went to school. This is from your immediate family, the church family, and people in the community. Also, we figured things out for ourselves. This is definitely the best basic education.

One very important thing we learned was Good Manners. In the 1920's and 1930's, we had respect for each other. Children were taught to respect each other and especially respect for adults. When we were learning to talk, some of the first words we were taught were thank you; please; pardon me; excuse me; yes, ma'm; and no, sir.

When a group was eating together, the adults went first, or the children walked with their parents, or came last in line. They did not rush to the front of the line and grab big pieces of chicken and other food with no intentions of eating it all. We did not leave the table unless everyone was leaving or we ask permission.

Men would always open the door for a woman and usually pull the chair out for a woman to sit down.

When an adult, and especially an elderly person, came into a room, the children would stand up and give them their seat. Men would do the same.

Most men wore felt hats; and when they came inside, they always took their hats off.

The women always offered visitors something to eat or drink after asking them if they would like to take off their coat or jacket.

We were taught it was very rude to interrupt someone when they were talking.

I wanted to please my family, my church family, and my community family. I wanted them to be proud of me. I think this helped us to develop a conscience. I truly believe if teenagers had a conscience and respect for others they would not be out killing each other. This training in good manners starts as a very young child.

It was a Happy Day when Daddy let me have a hoe with a short handle. We only hoed our larger crops (corn, beans and cabbage) three times, usually over two and a half to three months - mostly late May to late August. We would hoe in the cool of the day. After eating our mother's great lunch, we would take a long rest before we went back to the field. Daddy would say, "Don't get too hot. Go to the shade." My sisters would hoe so fast down a row, but I was so particular not to damage the plants and be sure I got every weed. They hoed twice as much as I did. They never figured out why I got to the field first in the morning. It was because I wanted to get where I had hoed before and would not be as many weeds because I left it in good shape.

Hoeing vegetables was not our only job but was the most time consuming. When we got ready to start planting things that would sprout in the ground, it would be after May 1st. Daddy would explain that we would be working in partnership with God. We thanked God for so many things, not just saying "Thank you, God, for this food."

We worked fewer hours daily, weekly and monthly compared to people on public jobs. In fact, I didn't think of it as work or labor. It was doing my part of the family business to have a good life. Mother and Daddy's work went on all year, but not the girls.

I did not enjoy, however, a number of other things. We didn't have electricity and used kerosene lamps. The lamp globes had to be washed often, at least every Saturday. If you turned the wicks up too high it would blacken the globes. My two older sisters, Josephine and Hazel, would have me wash the kerosene lamp globes. They convinced me that my hands were smaller and could get inside the globes.

They also had me washing our empty jars on canning day that had been stored away for most of the year. We had to carry the water up the hill from the spring and build a fire in the cook stove to heat the water. Then I washed the jars first in hot soapy water and rinsed them in hot water. Even though I didn't enjoy those chores, I did them well. Later in life I figured it out - my sisters were using me.

CHAPTER EIGHT

The School Years

My first formal schooling was at Otto Elementary, 1st grade, 1932-1933 through the 7th grade, 1938-1939. This was a two-room school built a few hundred feet from our house in our former garden spot. I could not tell stories about walking two miles in the snow. I think I was jealous of friends bringing little pails or bags of lunch. I crossed the schoolyard and went home for lunch.

The school was opened in 1932 and used through the 1939-1940 school year with two teachers. I attended the school every year it was in use except the last year. We had a well with a bucket on a rope. We let the bucket down into the well water and then we called it drawing the water up. I don't remember if we had the rope on a wheel or just pulled it up with our hands. We also had two outhouses, a wood-burning stove, and no electricity.

The former school where my sisters attended was across the Little Tennessee River. The public road went from the main highway through our bottomland, which flooded a lot during late winter and early spring. During this time, they could not have school. For years my parents had offered the school officials some land on the main highway for a con-solidated school, as several small schools in the community were getting very old. When the old school burned, they de-cided to build a two-room school on my parents' land. After another seven years, they got more of our land and built a large, stone, beautiful consolidated school. The WPA em-ployees built most of it.

I rode a school bus to attend Franklin High School. In the winter, the school bus was cold. I remember only a metal floor with no covering. It was ten miles on the main road, but we went up and down side roads so the trip was much longer. You could make a lot of good friends on these long rides. What a big change going from a two-room school to a high school! We only went through the 11th grade in high school and eight months per year. The 12th year was added to the elementary school in 1944, the year after my graduation. During high school, a lot of boys went into the service and several girls married boys going into the service and moved out of town with their husbands.

I remember two things about high school: as a freshman, I took typing. I had never laid a hand on a typewriter. At that time, they were not electric; and we had to hit the keys with a great force. I got behind in the first week. I decided I didn't like it for my daddy had taught me, "Don't do anything that you could not look back and be proud." Up until then, I had always been proud of what I did. I rode the first bus home, and during the school hours there was not an extra typewriter to use. No one in my community had a typewriter I could use to "catch-up". I hated typing and made the worst grade in my 11 years of school.

The other thing I remember about high school was Mrs. Green, my freshman English teacher, writing in my 1939-1940 autograph book. What she wrote gave me confidence all my life, and I would swear by it. I have met a lot of famous people, made lots of speeches, and had 69 years and 7 months of employment. I have walked into a lot of business meetings and have felt comfortable for I remembered to "Be what you is, and not what you ain't. If you ain't what you is, then you is what you ain't." by Hambone. I remembered I grew up where we spoke the Queen's English in Western North Carolina and not to try to talk and act otherwise.

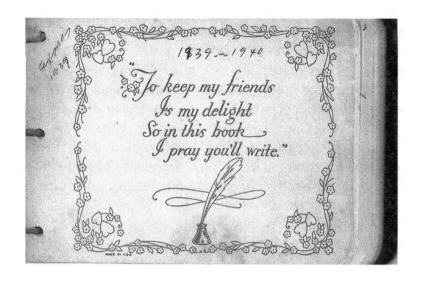

1939 — 1940

"To keep my friends
Is my delight
So in this book
I pray you'll write."

Off we go into the distant yonder,
    Climbing high into success;
Here we go -- ready to meet our future,
    Forward class -- give it our best!
Up we climb -- seeing our goals before us,
    So the world will all know
        We live -- and gain
        Or lose not -- in vain, 'cause
Nothing'll stop the '43 class!

Here's farewell to the swell classmates
    we lose and honor to the end,
To our friends we send our message
    of a cause that we'll defend.
We think of those who gave their all for us --
Then thanks we give, for their undying love and trust,
    Farewell to the swell old friends,
    we hail from Franklin High School.

Less than a month after I graduated from High School, I was in school with Western Union. I was just 17 years old and living by myself. Learning the Teletype wasn't as frightening as learning to use a typewriter, as the Teletype had only three rows of keys, all capitals. The numbers and symbols were under the capital letters. After I was shown how to use it, it was not a bad experience as the Teletype was electric.

I have another chapter about the rest of my 17th through 19th year of work and education. I am sure I learned more about things I needed to know and things that interested me in life the first year I worked at Western Union than I would have learned in four years of college. I would not exchange my experience for one million dollars or eight years in college.

CHAPTER NINE

Asbury Methodist Church

This is what I have been told and still believe: All the land for the early or progression of the church and the cemetery came from four generations of my family – from my great grandparents, grandparents, my parents, and my sister.

At various times, my great grandfather Bradley, sold land for five cents to $5 an acre to The Trustees of Methodist Episcopal South Church later to be known as Asbury Methodist Church. A log house was built of hickory logs, with the bark still on them, as a house for religious service and a school. About 25 years later, the church members built another house with hewed logs. This was replaced by an excellent frame building constructed for a church. That frame building burned in 1902, supposed to have caught fire from a defective flue. (I have the Franklin Press clippings about this church and the fire). After the fire, the members built the church shown in the picture showing the church built in 1902-03. This is what I call my church since I attended there until I was fourteen when, in 1940, a new brick church was built on my parents' property where we used to have a garden, and is still in use as of this writing. I only went to the new brick church for three years before I left home to go to work.

The bell from the old church was moved to the new church. At both the old and new churches, my daddy would ring the church bell about an hour before the service was to start. About ten minutes before we went into the church, he would ring it three times again, letting us know to stop talking and go inside. My mother would remind me to go to the outhouse, if necessary. Inside, we had to sit still and weren't to move, even if we thought we needed to go out. My mother would pinch my leg if I looked around or talked. WE WERE THERE TO WORSHIP AND TO LEARN in a place of reverence. My mother was hospitalized once for several days and my daddy took good care of us children. I recall going to the fields with him while he worked, and he took us to church. When Mother came back home, I told her I was glad she was home, but I was sorry she was going to be able to go to church "cause Daddy didn't pinch." She told that story on me many times.

Another time my daddy would toll the church bell was when someone died in the community. He would make the bell sound ding, dong, ding, dong in a mournful sound. That way everyone was notified someone had died. The men would come to the cemetery with their shovels and picks to dig the grave. Daddy didn't toll the bell for the number of years the person lived, since he didn't always know and didn't want to hurt anyone's feelings if he got it wrong. When he was getting ready to toll the bell, I would run up onto the hill, lie down on the grass where I could get a clear view of the sky. I wanted to watch as the person "went to heaven". I was young then and wondered, "If a person went to heaven, why did they have to dig the grave?" Church bells today are seldom used, hanging silent, no longer needed for the communication they used to provide.

We didn't have church every Sunday since we had a Circuit Preacher who took care of five different churches. We didn't have a printed schedule, but I have a later copy of one schedule listing Asbury as having services on the 2nd Sunday at 10:00 a.m. and on the 4th Sunday at 11:00 a.m. Even then it could be changed "because of weather conditions or for some other conditions beyond our control". Even without a preacher, the members of the church did a good job of conducting a service or just Sunday school in a very meaningful way. Everyone was like family, caring for each other nearly as much as our immediate family. We had our church family, community family, and relatives all looking out for us.

One of these memorable persons was Aunt Mary Curtis, 1878-1950. She was not my aunt, but 2nd cousin. We called everyone Uncle or Aunt when they were about 50 years old and older. Aunt Mary lived next to the Coweeta Laboratory and would walk with four or five grandchildren about eight miles round trip to the old Asbury Methodist Church. She would bring biscuits with something in them to eat while walking back home. Every Sunday, my daddy would invite them to go home with us for lunch. Occasionally they would. Everybody loved Aunt Mary.

We would have a week-long revival at Asbury Methodist Church, and Aunt Mary would get out in the aisle and shout and clap her hands when the preaching got real active. After she started, someone else would start shouting and clapping, too. But she would get it started. Our revivals were special for our congregation and neighboring churches. The visiting preacher and our pastor and their families would be invited to eat at a different home each day. The women would put on a "big spread" for the event.

Aunt Mary had nine children and lots of grandchildren. One of these grandsons, the late George Curtis, said his grandfather, Aunt Mary's husband, Julius Hightower Curtis, had the last funeral in the old Asbury Methodist Church in August 1940. The family thought the new church was completed enough for the funeral, but a committee voted against it.

What I remember most about the new church were the young CCC (Civil Conservation Corps) men on Sunday nights at Epworth League. They had to walk many miles round trip from the CCC Camp up at the Experimental Station. My mother cooked a lot for these young men for she knew it was hard on a lot of them to be away from their homes. They were 18-25 years of age making $30 per month, and $25 had to be sent back to their families at home only keeping $5 a month for themselves. If you go for a ride in the government-controlled parks, you are riding across the stone bridges, seeing stone walls, and walking across trails these young men built.

Back in those days, I was scared to get up before a crowd to speak. At 14, I became President of the Epworth League. I was soon not afraid because I was up before all those strangers, the CCC men. I haven't stopped talking since.

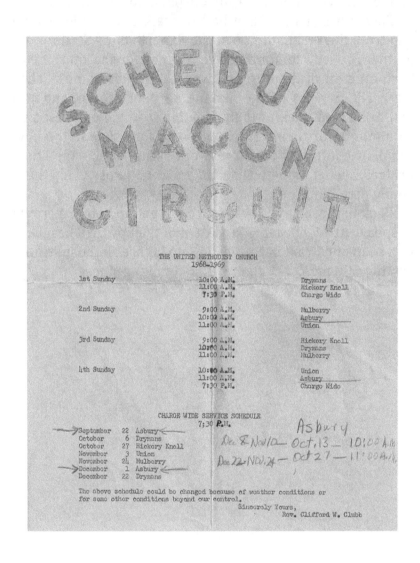

SCHEDULE MACON CIRCUIT

THE UNITED METHODIST CHURCH
1968-1969

1st Sunday	10:00 A.M.		Drymans
	11:00 A.M.		Hickory Knoll
	7:30 P.M.		Charge Wide
2nd Sunday	9:00 A.M.		Mulberry
	10:00 A.M.		Asbury
	11:00 A.M.		Union
3rd Sunday	9:00 A.M.		Hickory Knoll
	10:00 A.M.		Drymans
	11:00 A.M.		Mulberry
4th Sunday	10:00 A.M.		Union
	11:00 A.M.		Asbury
	7:30 P.M.		Charge Wide

CHARGE WIDE SERVICE SCHEDULE
7;30 P.M.

September	22	Asbury
October	6	Drymans
October	27	Hickory Knoll
November	3	Union
November	24	Mulberry
December	1	Asbury
December	22	Drymans

Asbury
Dec 8 Nov 10 — Oct. 13 — 10:00 A.M.
Dec 22 Nov 24 — Oct 27 — 11:00 A.M.

The above schedule could be changed because of weather conditions or
for some other conditions beyond our control.

Sincerely Yours,
Rev. Clifford W. Clubb

E-FRANKLIN

THE FRANKLIN PRESS

FRANKLIN. N. C., WEDNESDAY, JANUARY 15, 1902

Special Notices.

Items in this column five cents per or each item. In regular local column, ten cents per line for each issue. In words make about a line.

We regret to learn that Asbury Methodist church in Smith's Bridge Township was burned yesterday. The fire caught from the stove after services had been held and the congregation had dispersed.

Messrs. George and Charles Addington will leave to-morrow for a week's trip to Georgia.

Hotel Jarrett:—Geo. R. Rethurum, Jno. A. Hornsworth, J. B. Ensley, G. A. Bartlett.

The weather has been clear for

Editor Franklin Press: We have just learned from your excellent paper that Asbury church, located half a mile from Smith's Bridge on the Tennessee river, in Macon county, N. C., a Methodist church, was destroyed by fire two weeks ago.

Seventy five or eighty years ago, a log house, built of hickory logs, with the bark still on them, was erected near this place by the Methodist people, as a house for religious service and was used both as a church and school house.

I remember when I was a small boy, four or five years old, that my eldest sister took me to the school to see how I would like it. Before night I made great complaint and had to be taken home. When I grew up I took charge of a Sunday school there, and carried on the school quite successfully, with the following literature: The Bible, Webster's Spelling Book, and the Union Question Book.

Some twenty years later, a hewed log house was erected a short distance from this location, which was used instead of the old church. The old house of unhewed logs was then abandoned. Twenty five years ago, at the same place, the members of Asbury church erected an excellent frame building, completed and fitted up in every particular, as a church for the congregation to carry on their services in. This is the church that has just been destroyed by fire. The report is that it is supposed to have caught fire from a defective flue after the con-

Continued Next Page

that Rev. T. Bright had been arrested Monday at Sylva on account of his connection with the Amos Owens-Cherry tree affair.

T. J. Johnston, Esq., has moved his law office into the court house, occupying the room recently used

gregation had left after service. A large cemetery was located here where a great many of our friends and some relatives are buried. The loss of this church will be heavily felt by the congregation, that worshiped at this place. Our sympathies are extended to them.

In less than two miles from this church was our boyhood home, where we were brought up, and the loss makes me feel like I had lost my home church.

Dr. N. F. Howard,
Dahlonega, Ga.

Jan. 27, 1902.

CHAPTER TEN

Outbuildings On The Farm

Life on the Farm was centered on raising our own food and being good citizens in the community. In order to accomplish these tasks, we had our home and five or more outbuildings:

The **Smokehouse** was a few steps from the house. I don't know why it was called the smokehouse, as we never smoked our hog meat. Our meat was cured with salt, not smoke. The smokehouse was used for storage of the salted meat and other things.

The **Outhouse** was absolutely necessary. Sometimes it was a one holer, and sometimes a two-holer. If there were children in the family, there would be one seat lower than the others. Our prize possession for the outhouse was a Sears and Roebuck catalogue. We kept our outhouse as clean as possible, using ashes from the fireplace and wood-burning stove. Occasionally, we bought a bag of lime.

One of the hardest things I experienced when selling Mother's property was destroying the old outhouse. It took me several days to get it burned down. I did not want the Otto Community Development Association to have to destroy it. The bushes and weeds had grown up around the outhouse, and one side had fallen in. I tied papers on the end of a long stick, stuck a lit match to the papers, and reached in as far as possible. I was afraid to get too close because I was afraid the ground would give way and I would fall in. I was also afraid of snakes that may be around. This definitely marked the end of an era.

The **Chicken House** was another outbuilding. Oh! How Mother loved taking care of her chickens, eggs, and the building itself. There were roosting poles where we kept the droppings cleaned off the floor. There were nests attached to the wall about five feet off the floor. We would change the straw often in the nests. A hen would let us know when she was ready to "set" on her eggs. We didn't need to disturb these. Mother would add a few more eggs to make a nest full. The hen would set on these eggs for 21 days until they hatched. You have never seen anything more caring than a mother hen taking care of her baby chicks.

The **Barn** had a big wide hall and doors at both ends with lots of stalls on the sides down the middle. One room was an office and had tool storage. In the back of the barn would be a sheep pen and a door opening into one of the stalls where one sheep at a time would be driven into for shearing. The sheep would be put on a table and held down while being sheared. To help my daddy, we would hire someone who was experienced and had the tools for shearing. I would have to write a very long chapter to include everything my mother did with the wool from the time it left that table until we were wearing clothing she made.

There is a separate chapter about just the Spring and Springhouse since it was so important.

CHAPTER ELEVEN

Porches

Above: The view from our front porch

The front and back porches were as important as any room inside, except the bedrooms and kitchen. Except for cold weather months, we never considered entertaining our visitors inside the house. Friends felt welcome to stop on our front porch and rest after walking a long ways to the stores, post office, etc. that joined our land.

After I was grown and came back home for a visit, I remember two women at different times telling me that, when I was a toddler and I saw them coming down the road, I would run down to the highway expecting them to stop and visit on the porch. This made me happy to be remembered as a good hostess as a toddler. I still love for friends to visit me on my porch.

I may not describe fully the uses of our back porch, but I will try. There was a long table with an oilcloth cover where we prepared food for everyday cooking and canning. On the table was always a bucket of spring water with a dipper and a wash pan nearby for washing the hands and face. In the summer, it was hot in the kitchen as we used a wood-burning cook stove. We had several strings of beans drying into leather britches, peppers and other vegetables hanging on the wall to cure. We had several straight chairs, benches, clothesline, and stacks of wood for the stove and fireplace. The back porch was a perfect addition to the kitchen.

Also on the back porch, Daddy had his shaving equipment - leather strap for sharpening his razor, brush, shaving cup, and mirror for shaving.

I believe current architects, builders, and homeowners never lived in a home built prior to 1940. They do not know what a porch should be. If you can't sit in a rocking chair and not have to draw your feet up when someone walks in front of you, or you hit your head on the wall leaning back, then you are not comfortable.

If you can't seat people comfortably around a table to eat—why have it? A porch should be eight feet or wider. If not, it is just decoration so the front of your home will not look like a box. Today, you can drive around hundreds of homes in subdivisions and never see anyone enjoying their porches. WHAT A SHAME!

These are two homemade chairs that were left in my mother's home when she entered the nursing home. We had several chairs like these on the porches, in the eating area, around the fireplace and in the bedrooms. I believe these would be 100 years old or older. I remember them all my life and do not remember by parents buying new ones.

The frames would not wear out but the seats had to be re-canned. This was a work of art, especially from the big hands of mountain men. They used white oak splits, cane, stripes of hickory bark, or a rope made from corn shucks. Ours was white oak splits. The best time to harvest any timber you will be working with is in the fall or winter, when the sap is down. This will cause less warping. Then they let it dry several months and make it into perfect splits, same width and thickness splits. Before starting the weaving of the chair bottom they would soak the splits in cold water at least a half of an hour to make them more pliable and cause them to tighten on the chair frame when dry.

Yes it was called weaving and such delicate work for a man's big hands. I wish I could watch it one more time.

CHAPTER TWELVE

Branch, Spring and Springhouse

Above: From the top is where the Dripping Springs was located

As a child, I enjoyed a little stream flowing into a branch (which is also called a little stream but not big enough to be called a creek) starting near the top of our mountain, known as "The Little Mountain", where there was a huge rock and on one corner was water dripping off. We named the rock "The Dripping Spring Rock." We could slide down the rock like today where there are water slides. Also, around the rock were really good blackberries, chestnuts, and chinquapins. The view was "out of this world". If we said we were going to the Dripping Rock, everyone knew we were hiking to the top of the mountain. We never went alone. It was fun hiking to the top of the mountain.

In the coves below were other little springs meandering around and joining the water starting from the Dripping Rock to make a good size branch going by the barn, by our main spring, and springhouse. The spring was where my grandparents and my parents got their water. One night there was a big windstorm. The next morning, above the spring they had been using, they saw where a wild cherry tree had been uprooted and underneath there was a bigger spring with rocks stacked perfectly surrounding fast-flowing water. Grandfather said God and the Indians had previously made this spring. I had a mystical feeling, one I can't describe, when I tried to picture someone building the wall around the spring and then hiding it by covering it up. In my child's mind, I thought perhaps the spring was sacred to the Indians. I always thought and believed that when the Indians had to leave, they covered dirt over their beautiful stacked stone and rock spring to hide it and let the water continue to flow below it. They covered it up because it belonged to them. My grandfather had acquired a land grant through the Governor of North Carolina the State had obtained from the Treaty with the Indians. I am not sure this was the exact land, but I like to think it was where our spring was located.

When I was a young child, I adopted the upkeep of our spring, springhouse, and the grounds around it. This area and the church were my two most reverent places I visited. I kept the spring and the waterway through the springhouse clean and all the weeds cleared off the land between the branch and springhouse until it went into the branch. Daddy said I was cleaning so much nothing would be left! I wanted it to be as beautiful as possible and as clean as someone's living room when they were expecting the preacher to visit. I would look at the water coming out of the spring and wonder, "If I followed the water, where would it end?"

So many things depended on a good spring - all our drinking water, washing clothes, taking a bath, washing the dishes, in our food we cooked, and on and on. Since we did not have any electricity for a refrigerator, we kept everything we wanted to keep cool in the springhouse where it was nice and cool. The water flowed through the springhouse where we kept our milk, butter, buttermilk, and vegetables. In the winter, we kept churns, or some people called them crocks, of kraut, pickled beans, hominy, and blanched apples in there. In warm weather, we churned our butter between the branch and the spring where it was so tranquil churning and churning, listening to the branch water ripple and the birds sing. I liked to churn.

The highway was a few hundred feet away from the spring and a lot of people would stop to get a cold, sweet, clean drink of water after walking miles to the stores, post office, depot, and John Conley's blacksmith shop at Otto. Otto was surrounded on three sides by our farm. We left a big dipper hanging on the springhouse wall for everyone to use. They didn't worry about drinking after each other.

The Spring was a reverent place for me. I wish I could explain it in words. I can't. I can, however, tell you how I enjoyed the little wild flowers along the water from the spring into the branch. I can tell you how thankful I was for the continuous water freely given to us with no fear it would stop. I can tell you how I thought about the people who built the walls around the spring. I can tell you how I wondered where the water would be the next day. I can tell you how nice and cool it was to sit down there and churn good, fattening butter. I can tell you how happy I was for people to stop to get a drink of water. I can tell you how great it was to take a teacup in the winter and mash it down in a churn of kraut and get a cup of the kraut juice and drink it or for Mother to send me to get some beans or apples to cook.

The rocks were still there when we sold the property exactly as when I first saw it. Not a rock was out of place after more than 100 years. Most of all I had lots to thank God for, even the little blue flowers by the stream. Now, it is a man-made pond that makes me sick with no resemblance to work done at least 100 years ago.

The back of the house. We carried water up this hill.

CHAPTER THIRTEEN

Washday and Ironing

The spring was important for our drinking water, as well as the animals. However, one of our biggest uses of water was for washday usually once a week, on Monday. Our water was carried from the spring across the branch. A huge pot was filled with water, and then a fire was built to heat the water. The clothes were sorted: whites and coloreds. While the water was heating, the clothes were scrubbed in a big tub on a washboard using homemade lye soap, or we used Octagon store-bought soap. This took a lot of scrubbing on the washboard. Then we rung out the clothes and put them in the boiling water. Mother could make lye soap, but it was very hard on her hands using ashes and lye.

While boiling, we would punch the clothes around for 15 minutes or more with a wooden paddle and a broomstick, pressing the clothes against the pot. Using the broomstick, we held the clothes up above the tub to let the dirty water drip out. This was a steaming hot job for an adult. Then the clothes were transferred to another big zinc tub filled with cold water. The clothes were rinsed around. White clothes were put into another tub of water with bluing in it to make them whiter. Next, if they needed starch, we would put them in a smaller tub or dishpan of water with dissolved starch.

After that whole hot process, we hung them out on a clothesline in hopes of getting them dry that day. The whites were hung in the sun for bleaching. The colored clothes were hung in the shade to avoid fading. PLUS the outside air gave them all a fresh smell. Before the evening dampness fell, we would gather the clothes, folding as we went.

Ironing was done on Tuesday. The starched clothes had to be dampened for easier ironing. We had to build the fire in all four seasons in the cook stove to heat the irons. I did not like to iron. In particular, I did not like ironing my father's blue denim shirts and overalls since it was hard to get the iron hot enough for the heavy cloth. I did not want to be ashamed of his appearance if they were not ironed nicely.

When I got married, I told my husband the only reason I would want a pre-nuptial agreement was to state that I would not iron his shirts. He said, "I don't want you to iron my shirts, because I stop by the cleaners as I come home on Fridays to drop off this week's dirty laundry and pick up last week's."

During the week before our first anniversary, he did several things unusual. He did not stop at the cleaners to drop off and pick up his laundry. Sunday was our first anniversary and I told him, lovingly, "I will do your laundry." He said, "No, I have done it lots of times." I thought, "Thank goodness." Monday morning, at age 46, as he was leaving to go to work, he had a heart attack. When I first saw him at the hospital, I almost had a heart attack. He had only ironed down the front, the cuffs and collar of the shirt he was wearing since that was all that would show from under his dress jacket. Believe me! The shirt was not wash and wear. I still wonder what the hospital staff thought of his wife?

I may not have recovered from my embarrassment, but he recovered from this heart attack. He returned to work and tried to prove he wasn't sick. He won awards for going over his company allotments, even driving the difficult mountain route until another heart attack made him a shut-in from 1967-81.

Years later, my mother was visiting me; and she wanted to press her clothes immediately after unpacking. "Sorry, Mother. I loaned my friend my iron." When Mother was leaving, she took a $10 bill and slapped it down on the table and said, "If this is not enough money to buy an iron, I see you have some Green Stamps. I won't come back unless you have an iron!"

GRANDMA'S OLD-FASHIONED WASH "RECEIPT"

Speaking of doing the family wash, I'd like to pass on "Grandma's Receipt for doing the family wash" in the good old days. We would hardly recommend this routine for saving Grandma's energy though. This is an authentic "receipt" in its original spelling as it was written out for a bride four generations ago:

1. Bild a fire in back yard to heet kettle of rain water
2. Set tubs so smoke won't blow in eyes if wind is pert.
3. Shave one hold cake lie sope in bilin water.
4. Sort things, make three piles. 1 pile white. 1 pile cullord. 1 pile work britches and rags.
5. Stur flour in cold water to smooth, then thin down with bilin water.
6. Rub dirty spots on boards, scrub hard, then bile. Rub cullord, but don't bile – just rench and starch.
7. Take white things out of kettle with broom stick

handle, then rench, blew, and starch.
8. Spred tee towels on grass.
9. Hang old rags on fence.
10. Pore rench water on flower bed.
11. Scrub porch with hot sopey water.
12. Turn tubs upside down.
13. Go put on clean dress – smooth hair with side combs – brew cup of tea – set and rest and rock a spell and count blessins.

Author Unknown

Growing Our Food

We had lots to eat by growing our own vegetables that we canned or preserved in whatever way we could. There were butter beans and several kinds of green beans which could be cooked with a piece of meat, or were pickled and a churn full put in the spring house for winter use. Green beans were broken into small pieces and strung on a thread and hung up to dry (tough as leather giving them the name of Leather

Britches, but after soaking them overnight and cooking for a long time, they were satisfying in your tummy).

We had different kinds of peas – green peas, black-eyed peas, and field peas. The field peas were picked when they were mature and the husk was dry. On a windy day, we put the peas on a big piece of old cloth, such as a sheet, then beat the husk with a stick or paddle and flipped them up in the air to let the wind blow away the husk. Then the peas would drop back onto the cloth. After several times flipping them up in the wind, the husk was gone with the wind. My mother would cook them with a piece of cured pork (called streaked meat), and we ate it with corn bread.

There was sweet corn and field corn. Further on I will tell about all the different ways corn was used, but here is where I am telling about how we ate it. We enjoyed creamed corn, pickled corn, hominy, and corn on the cob. Mother would say, "Go get the corn. I am starting the water to boil." Now you would call that fresh corn. We grew several rows of popcorn and shelled it ourselves. We made our own popper with screen wire and a broomstick, and popped the corn over the fire in the fireplace.

We grew several varieties of tomatoes. We had them fresh, canned, and put into soup. Back then, we never thought of frying them green.

We had Irish potatoes served baked, fried or mashed. I still call them mashed potatoes; however, I use an electric beater and whip them, so they are not mashed potatoes now. We also had sweet potatoes. The best way to bake sweet potatoes was in a Dutch oven on the hearth of the fireplace, placing fire coals on top and bottom. Or they could be fried or boiled. My mother also could make the best sweet potato cobbler. I have not found anyone outside of the area where I grew up who has ever heard of Sweet Potato Cobbler. I still make it but never as good as my mother's. I make the excuse that she had fresh, homemade butter and whole milk right from the cow. Every time my nephew, Edd Dowdle, visits, he wants me to cook sweet potato cobbler.

Onions were grown, either the little fresh, green onions or the matured onions that lasted all winter. There were turnips that we ate raw, boiled or fried, or just the greens.

Cabbage was eaten raw, fried, boiled, slaw, or kraut. We would make a crock full of kraut and put it in the springhouse for the winter. I would take a cup and mash down the kraut and get a good, cold cup of kraut juice. After I left home and would come home for a visit, Mother would say, "What do you want to eat?" She knew I would always say, "Fried cabbage." She would chop it up very fine and fry some streaked meat, then put the cabbage in for just a little while. Then we would eat it with buttermilk cornbread.

We grew our own peanuts, carrots, and squash of different kinds, radishes, beets, peppers, cucumbers, rhubarb, greens of all kinds, blackberries, huckleberries, mulberries, persimmons, and peaches. We bought our canning peaches when a man would bring them up from Georgia. We gathered hazelnuts, chinquapins and chestnuts until the blight killed all the trees.

We grew our own wheat for wheat bread, corn for corn-bread, rye for rye bread. Some of my happy days were going with my daddy to one of the two water-ground mills we had in our community. We would load up the wagon on a day when the ground was wet and we couldn't work in the fields. Other people would be out in their yards or on their porches; we would stop to talk before going on with our corn, wheat, or rye. It did not cost us money to have the corn, rye, and wheat ground at the mill. The miller would take his toll in corn, rye, or wheat, known as the bartering system.

We would just make a day of it. So enjoyable! When we cooked rye bread, we made apple cider to go with it.

We had apples to eat raw, boiled, baked, fried, jelly, apple butter, marmalade, or make a churn of blanched (some people called them bleached apples for they would turn white for a year). Mother would peel and slice the apples and put several inches in the bottom of the churn, then put hot fire coals in a shallow container with sulfur sprinkled on top. Cover and leave over night. Do the same thing over and over until the churn was full. The apples would stay nice for a year. Just think of having apple pie in January.

We had bees to give us honey, and we picked wild grapes, and made molasses from cane we planted. We had cows to supply milk so we could churn our butter giving us buttermilk. And we made cottage cheese.

There were our chickens, ducks, and the eggs. Other meats we had would be pork, rabbits, squirrels, raccoons, or fish out of the Little Tennessee River that ran around the east side of our farm. Daddy wasn't a hunter, but he would kill the squirrels that ate his corn. Mother used to make dumplings to go with squirrel meat. Daddy would let hunters and trappers go up on the mountain and trap raccoons. The raccoons would be put in a cage for two weeks to feed them to get some of the wild taste out of their meat. Raccoon was better and more meat than a chicken or duck. When cold weather came around, local farmers would come by and sell beef. I can still smell that meat cooking on the stove and sweet potatoes cooking on the fireplace.

By winter, if we had not canned or preserved all of the food, we would dig a hole in a bank, line it with straw, and store apples, turnips, Irish and sweet potatoes, heads of cabbage, and other things. A small door was used to cover the opening.

In the spring, when we got tired of digging stuff out of the straw and eating canned goods, we were happy to see some wild greens come up. The first things I remember to come up were field creases in the field where the corn had been planted the previous year. This was called green-up time. When the creases got the size of a dinner plate, we would cut it, parboil it, and then fry streaked meat, and cook the creases in the grease. Then a little later, the poke sallet would come up, giving us a fresh supply of food. We would parboil the poke sallet, drain it, and then cook it again in a skillet with fatback meat. We would boil eggs to put on top of the poke sallet. Sure tasted good!

From a little grain of corn:

I believe corn was the most valuable seed that could be planted for humans and animals. We fed our animals: hogs, cattle, chickens, sheep, and horses everything produced from corn – from the kernels of corn to the leaves known as fodder. We used most of the corn stalks for roadbeds.

For humans, we ate corn in so many ways. We couldn't wait to get our first corn on the cob about July 4th. Mother would have the water boiling and tell us to hurry out to the garden and get some corn. Now, that was fresh corn. We ate it on the cob or cut it off the ear and then scraped the cob to get the milky juice for creamed corn cooked in an iron skillet. We would roast the whole ear in the shuck. On a cold night, nothing was better than a bowl of corn mush or what was sometimes called porridge. We preserved corn by canning or pickling.

We would spend all day at the wash pot cooking dried corn kernels to make hominy. Then we would can it or put it in a churn and keep it all winter in the springhouse.

Now let's think of how many ways corn shucks were used: bed ticks which are now called mattresses, dolls, napkin rings, bracelets, women's hats, men's hat bands, lamp shades, baskets, pleated and braided pocketbooks, ropes, cords, horses' harnesses, bridles, collars, the most comfortable chair bottoms, and beds for animals.

We could not live without corn bread made from real water-ground cornmeal. Some folks ate it three times a day. Corn was eaten in a variety of ways: in a big iron skillet, spoon bread, corn sticks, corn muffins, cracklin' corn bread, johnnycakes, corn pone cakes, hoe cakes, pancakes, or a bowl of corn mush. I also enjoyed Mother cooking corn bread in a Dutch oven on the hearth of the fireplace. She would keep plenty of hot coals on top and bottom of the pan to make a thick, crunchy crust and nice and soft inside.

Nothing feels as good on an ache or pain as a corn-meal poultice. Mother would put corn meal in hot water to make a mush, then put the mush in an old cloth and roll it up. The poultice would stay warm for a long time. She would scrape the corn meal off the cloth and save it a few hours and repeat it again. An old cloth had to be thrown away for you could not wash the starch out of it. Thank goodness, today you can put the cloth and corn meal in the microwave over and over and not have to scrape it out.

What can you add to this list of what a little grain of corn can provide? Go ask your grandparents. What more could we want; we felt we were rich. We may not have had money, but we never felt slighted or poor.

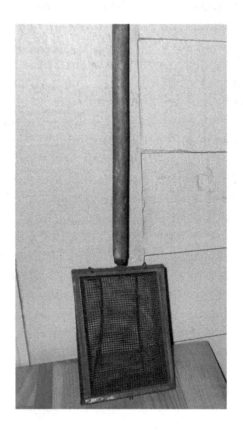

Another way to eat corn, popcorn. Pictured above is our popcorn popper.

CHAPTER FIFTEEN

Other Crops - Tobacco

The men raised chewing tobacco and twisted it in tight twists to carry in their pockets. They would bite off a piece and chew it. My daddy raised a little patch of chewing tobacco in the garden. He would not let his girls touch it for he was afraid we might like the smell and try to use it ourselves. After the leaves matured, he would completely dry or cure the leaves on a rack. On a rainy day, the extra moisture made it easier for him to work it into neat twists to carry in his pocket. He never used snuff.

A lot of men smoked a pipe. Some men would make and smoke corncob pipes. For their pipes, they would use tobacco that was dried and crumbled small enough to fill into their pipes. If the men used snuff, they were called Snuff Jaw Packers or Snuff Sniffers. Some elderly ladies would also smoke corncob pipes. I don't remember anyone smoking cigarettes.

The women in my community of Otto dipped snuff. My mother would mix hers with about one fourth flour and put some in a little metal snuffbox. When she went outside, she carried it in her apron pocket. She would put the snuff behind her lower lip and hold it for hours. We would buy the snuff for her at the store, but we never saw her put it behind her lip.

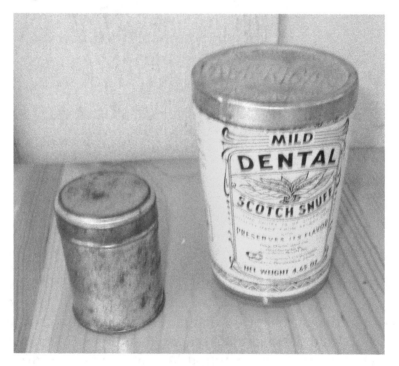

In the late 30's, I think about 1938, a family came to Otto from Madison County, North Carolina, a tobacco-growing county. They made an agreement with my daddy to make him a lot of money raising Burley Tobacco. Daddy would have to build a tobacco-drying barn with a lot of poles inside for hanging and drying the tobacco. The barn would not be worth much for anything else. Daddy built the barn at great expense.

The next year, the Agricultural Adjustment Administration passed a law to have quotas on tobacco allotments. Since my daddy had only one year of sales, he was only allotted one fourth of an acre. Needless to say, the family who came to grow the tobacco had to return to Madison County; and Daddy was stuck with a tobacco barn, poles, and vacant space.

I recall the time my French teacher, Mrs. Greene, asked me if I would help one of my friends study for our French mid-term exam. My friend was to spend the night with us. Mother banked the fire in the fireplace before going to bed. We wanted to study near the warm hearth. There by the hearth was my mother's snuffbox. Oh! No! We didn't! Yes, we did... We put some snuff between our lip and gums. Just a few minutes later we were both so very, very sick. We went out in the December weather and rolled on the frozen ground. I thought I was going to die! NO MORE TOBACCO PRODUCT FOR ME.

In the first class after Christmas Holidays, Mrs. Greene came walking toward me with the exam papers. I was so scared and maybe a little panicky for I had not studied myself. She said, "Congratulations, Lotus, you made the highest grade in the class." My friend also passed that French exam. I was so happy for her. She had a very successful life and it did not have anything to do with French. We never told anyone that we thought we were going to heaven that night we studied together.

CHAPTER SIXTEEN

Chickens and Their Cousins (Ducks & Geese)

Chickens were a big part of our life. Mother and Daddy knew how many hens to have per rooster so the eggs would fertilize and hatch baby chickens. Most of the time, Mother would know when the hen wanted to set. She would put extra eggs under her. In 21 days, the eggs would start to crack open with baby chickens. Some hens wanted to hide their nest outside the chicken house. We were always looking for a nest hidden on the ground. If that hen had not already started setting on her eggs, we would bring them in the chicken house, add a few more to her nest, and hope she would continue to set on them until they hatched. Seldom could a hen set on a nest outside for long enough to hatch the eggs without some wild animal eating her eggs.

When we gathered eggs from the chicken house, there was no need to test those eggs for freshness. However, if we found eggs outside, we would put those eggs in a pan of water to see if they would lie completely on the bottom of the pan. If they floated, they were too old to eat. I still can't get out of the habit. When store-bought eggs are nearing the expiration date, I will put them in water to see if they stay on the bottom. Old habits don't just die hard; sometimes they live forever.

We kept our chicken house very clean. All the droppings were used as fertilizer in the garden. We didn't waste anything. The straw in the nest was always clean.

My mother could cook the best fried chicken, make gravy, and bake biscuits. We ate eggs fried, scrambled, boiled, and deviled. We needed eggs in so many things we cooked, especially cakes and puddings.

If we needed something from the store and didn't have the cash, we could always take chickens and eggs to trade. The storekeepers were glad to get them as a man came around on a regular basis to buy them from the storekeeper. I remember one time when my mother was sending my sister and me to the store with a chicken. We had a hard time finding a string to tie its legs. When we came home from the store, I was crying. Mother said, "What is the matter?" I said, " Mr. Mozely kept our string, and I wanted it back." Mr. Mozely was the storekeeper.

We tried raising ducks. They lived in and on the side of the branch. They slept on the ground and laid their eggs on the ground. They were a good target for wild animals and were often killed. This made us very sad. My sisters liked duck eggs, which were larger than a chicken egg and very rich.

Once I was invited to go with my neighbors, Mr. and Mrs. Brown, nearly to the end of Tessentee Road to Granny Brown's birthday celebration. Her home looked like what I thought the Garden of Eden would look like. She had a little lake or a big pond where the children were playing. She also had several beautiful geese. Immediately, when I went down to the lake/pond, a big gander came from behind me and bit my leg. I was probably four or five years old. Oh, my goodness, I was scared beyond words. Needless to say, I stayed on the porch most of the rest of the day. Granny Brown was so sorry. In a few weeks I received a goose-down pillow that she and Nellie Clouse had picked thousands of down feathers from the geese to make my pillow. That pillow is probably 85 years old.

Our parents would never let us kill a black snake. They especially thought snakes were their friends around the corncrib because snakes kept the rats away. One day when I was home for a visit, Mother went to gather her eggs. When I heard her screaming, I looked out the door. She had a long stick beating something on the ground. My mild, caring mother's face was red; and she was MAD. I ran down there, and she was beating a black snake. As evidence, there was still an egg in the snake's throat. She had previously told me her hens were not laying eggs very well. She then realized the hens weren't at fault. I would not have believed this if I had not been there to see and hear my mother. Say no more, this was her first time to kill a black snake. Added to this, the foxes were killing mother's chickens. She was so sad.

After my daddy died, the fencerows around the barn and other buildings began to look rough with weeds and vines growing up. Around our chicken house didn't look the same, either.

CHAPTER SEVENTEEN

Hog Killin'

I don't believe we could have survived if we had not raised hogs and lived on the meat. We let them graze on the grass and fed them plenty of corn. The hogs were fed scraps of food from our meals and liquids we called "slop".

In olden days, folks let their hogs roam in the mountains or open range to eat things like chestnuts and chinquapins, grass, and much more. They said that acorns gave the meat a bad taste and altered the consistency of the fat for the lard. Chestnuts made good-tasting meat and good lard. In the fall, a hog roundup was a special time. They would bring them into the farm and feed them corn up to a month to get the wild taste out before killing them. However, our hogs were raised in a large hog lot where they had plenty of room, grass to eat, and water to drink.

Hog-killin' day was a special community time for men and women. In the fall after several good, heavy frosts, the men would help Daddy. I can't tell about the actual killing of the hogs. Daddy would send the girls into the house while this was being done. Later, I understood there were two ways to accurately kill a hog. Either way, it was a bloody mess!

Daddy would have lots of water to the boiling point when the men got there. They scalded the hair and the skin so they could scrap all the hair off the hogs. If the water was too hot, the hair was harder to scrape off. They would tie the hog on a gallows (two upright poles and a crossbar). More hot water was poured on the skin where they had missed the hair and the rest would be scraped off. After the hog is completely cleaned and washed out, the gutted carcass is taken down, for it is ready to be cut up.

The men would cut up the meat and take certain pieces to the smoke house for salting and curing. We had a smoke-house, but I don't believe we ever smoked our meat, just salted it for curing, and canned it. We never saved the intestines for the chitins'. We never saved the eyes. They were really hard to remove. I believe we saved the rest. I can't name all the parts, but I remember two big pots: a sausage pot would be started from the trimmings of mostly lean meat, for grinding into sausage, and a lard pot to save the fat trimmings for lard and cracklin' meat.

I will probably not name all the parts to be cut up for curing with salt and the rest canned, cooked over the next few days, or to be eaten or given to the friends that helped. I recall the men would leave the shoulders, hams, streaked middlin' meat (similar to bacon), and the jowls to be salted for curing. Everyone took meat home. Then this would all be repeated in a few days at someone else's home.

The wives would come to help Mother in the kitchen to can the meat. I remember our canning tenderloin, sausage, cracklin's, ribs, backbones, liver for good liver mush, part of the head for souse meat, and brains that we cooked with eggs.

The kitchen was overcrowded with all the women there to help. My job was to grind and grind the sausage meat over in the corner out of the way. Then the ground sausage was made into little balls, fried, and canned. The jar was turned upside down so the grease would settle into the top of the upside down jar and this would seal it. THERE HAS BEEN NO BETTER SAUSAGE THAN CANNED FRESH SAUSAGE.

We usually saved the pot of fat pieces to be boiled into lard and cracklin's the next day. This was a messy day. We put the lard into buckets and canned the cracklin's for good cracklin' corn bread later in the winter.

I am sure I have not given a complete picture of hog killin' day, but you have fun and fill in the blanks or get your grandparents to fill in the blanks. My friends in Hancock County, Tennessee, Mitch Holt and his sisters, Mary and Linda, still raise their hogs and do the same thing we did when I was small. Mitch raised two hogs in 2014 and brought me cured ham, ham hocks, and some canned sausage and cracklin's. Thank you, Mitch.

CHAPTER EIGHTEEN

Making Molasses

Some people call it sorghum, some molasses, some cane syrup. Whichever you call it, molasses making was a community affair, just like killin' the hogs or corn- shuckin' time. It was like a family reunion. Instead of family, it was a community reunion with the same people as last year and maybe more.

For each farm to have a molasses mill was too expensive with the boiler box or vat, wood furnace, and roller mill to be pulled around by a horse to squeeze the juice out of the cane. I have heard of portable mills that went from farm to farm and charged one fourth of the molasses as their fee. I believe our permanent mill in our pasture was the only one in Smithbridge Township. Farmers would bring wagons full of cane stalks from miles away and "make a day of it".

There is a lot of work and "know how" before molasses could be made. Daddy would only plant the seeds he had saved from last year in certain fields. The soil had to be just right. We planted several seeds in a hill about a foot apart. After God tended to their sprouting up, we would thin the plants and leave two or three per hill. Daddy said they needed to have sunlight and rain water so they would grow thick and strong. If the stalks were skinny and tall, they would not have the right juice when they matured.

A few days before the molasses making started, there was a lot of work to be done. I am afraid I can't tell it all, but I can share some of it. All the parts had been stored for the year except the rocked wall of the furnace. The boiler box, or vat, is cleaned and put on the furnace stand. Wood is cut for the many days of fire building. A good fire has to be built then burned down to coals so the smoke smell or taste doesn't taint the new molasses. If the fire gets too hot, someone has to put water on it to tame it down. The wooden paddle is located for scraping the vat so the molasses doesn't stick to the boiling box. The handmade skimmer is found, or a new one is made with a metal end and perforated holes so the juice will run out and leave the foam on the skimmer. A broomstick is used for a handle. A hole is dug next to the furnace where the foam is thrown out off the skimmer.

John Rice Irwin's
Museum of Appalachia
U.S. 441 and Tenn. 61, Norris, Tenn. 37828

While Oat Stooksbury feeds the sorghum into the cane mill, Elmer Sherwood leads the mule round and round in the endless process required in making molasses. In addition to the 20,000 items on display, many pioneer activities such as this are carried on.

Museum is one mile from Interstate 75 - Norris exit, 15 miles north of Knoxville.

Phone (615) 494-7680

Pub. by Stonecraft, 1510 Scenic Drive, Maryville, Tenn. 37801

post card

— Photo by Dean Stone
99200-C

dp DEXTER PRESS, INC.
WEST NYACK, NEW YORK

The mill and the rollers are cleaned and oiled. The long rein pole, or sweeper, is brought to the mill and attached. Usually wooden kegs are soaked in water several days to swell the lumber and keep them from leaking when the juice from the mill and the rollers flows into them through the first straining cloth. Before the juice is taken to the vat to boil, it has to be strained again through another cloth so lots of cloth has to be available. This is only part of the preparation. When the process starts, a lot of people have to be ready at their specific jobs, such as: tending the horse, loading the mill, removing the squeezed cane, bringing the juice to the vat.

The vat had several sections. I am sure it took a watchful eye to keep it moving. Everyone wanted my mother to be the skimmer, watching over the boiling juice, keeping the flow of the juice through the dividers until it came out the other end as molasses. She made all the rest of the preparations worth all the effort.

Molasses-making time was in late September to early October when the seeds are red and firm and before a hard freeze. The seeds are cut off and some are saved for next year's crop. The rest were fed to the chickens. We would then strip the leaves off the stalks for fodder, or silage, for the livestock. Then the stripped stalks were cut off at the bottom and loaded neatly onto the wagon to go to the molasses mill.

My mother being so involved caused me a lot of unhappiness. When I was pre-school, and my sisters were in school, I had my mother to myself. She was always at home, in the garden, the wash place, or in the barn. I was always with her. However, at molasses-making time, she was up in the pasture at the mill, taking care of everyone else and ignoring me! I didn't like staying up at the mill all day, either. I especially didn't like the yellow jackets that hung around the processing area, or to see the horse going around and around the mill all day. This molasses making lasted two weeks or more.

I was a good child most of the time. One time, however, Uncle Hessie Carr Smith was waiting while Mother was doing his skimming. He had two large, clean, and shiny tin buckets waiting to be filled. I put one foot in each of those buckets. Someone told my mother, and she hollered at me for she didn't want to leave her skimming job. I just stood there and acted as though I didn't hear her. She hollered again. Again, I didn't hear her. She left her skimming job, came over, and jerked my feet out of those buckets, and spanked me in front of all those people. My feelings were hurt more than the spanking. I only remember one spanking and one ankle switching in my life. I had probably learned from watching my sisters' misbehaving. I will never forget the times they both were disciplined!

Daddy said the hardest job he had on the farm was making my mother's breakfast biscuit and the molasses run out at the same time. I can just see it – a little biscuit left on his plate or a little molasses left. One without the other was not good.

CHAPTER NINETEEN

Store-Bought Items

In the 1920's and 1930's, I'd like to think we were self-sufficient; however, there were a few things we could not make or raise on the farm.

Matches were one thing we absolutely were unable to do without. There were no boy scouts in the family to know how to start a fire. We used matches to light lamps, lanterns, start a fire in the fireplace, light the kitchen cook stove for cooking and under the wash pot and many other things. If you had only one match left and had a lamp, candle, and lantern, which one would you light first? Look on the bottom of another page for my answer.

A lot of kerosene was needed for the lamps and lanterns. I wish I could remember all the things my daddy did with kerosene. I know he would use kerosene and steel wool to scrape rust off his tools.

Sugar had to be bought even though Mother used a lot of honey and molasses as a substitute for store-bought sugar. Of course we always needed salt, black pepper, baking powder, and vanilla flavoring. We needed Octagon soap to wash the clothes, and usually we had facial and hand soap.

We had to buy Mother's snuff. She would mix flour with it to make it last longer.

In the summer, we bought lard since what we made in the fall wouldn't last the whole year. Lard would have gone bad anyway even if it had lasted that long since we didn't add any preservatives.

I NEVER worried about our being able to pay for these things. My mother and daddy never went in debt one penny for anything. On the day we needed something from the store, we had plenty of chickens and eggs to trade. The storeowners liked that for there was a truck driver who had a regular route to pick them up, so the storeowners made money on the chicken and eggs.

CHAPTER TWENTY

Farm Finances

I never worried about cash. We always seemed to have a little when we needed it. We didn't have any monthly bills. We had an annual bill of property tax. My parents would "put back" money in a jar all year to be sure and have the tax money. Every time we made some cash, part of it would go to the church. As I have mentioned several times, if we needed something such as salt or sugar from the store, and didn't have cash, we had chicken and eggs to trade.

Our largest cash crop was green beans and the second was cabbage. We picked the beans three times for commercial sales. A big truck from Florida was always there with three men in it to test our beans early in the morning before we started to pick. The men would walk into our field with their panama straw hats (today I would call them the mafia, I didn't know the word then) and break two or three beans open. If they saw a sign of a bean and not all jelly, they would turn down the whole field of beans. If the buyers turned us down, it was a big loss to my parents. My daddy would say he was so sorry for the Florida people who had to eat beans without any beans in them. There was just the hull and jelly.

If this picking was turned down, we would give the beans away or can a lot of them, but they were not as good because we usually canned beans with a lot of little beans in the hull. We still had to pay the pickers, our neighbors, 15 cents a bushel to remove this picking so the next beans would be ready in about a week. This first picking was usually the best and most profitable. The only reason we would miss the proper day to pick was if it rained the day before.

Aunt Lid Dryman, one of the oldest pickers, wore a big long skirt and apron. She would go through the field as fast as a bat. She never left until she had picked ten bushels. That was $1.50 for the day. I could never pick more than three bushels per day since I was so particular not to damage a new bloom or a small bean. Aunt Lid didn't care; she was thinking of her ten bushels. Of course, she wasn't my aunt, but we gave every person a little older than us Uncle and Aunt for respect.

In the winter when Daddy was not working in the fields, he made money by hewing crossties for the railroad. All crossties were made with an axe, not a machine. He would hew all four sides until they were smooth.

Before the dogs killed our sheep, we made money selling sheep and wool. After the sheep were sheared, it was easy to sell the raw wool without doing anything to it.

My mother loved little calves. When her cow had a baby, she would buy a male calf from someone in the community and raised two calves. Most people wanted to keep their female calves but would sell their male calves. After a few months, she would sell them for veal.

We had lots of walnut trees, probably 20 to 25. In the fall, most children went to school with brown hands, as we had been picking up black walnuts to spread out to dry, so we could later hull them. Then we put them out to dry again in a place so the squirrels could not steal them. In the winter, Mother had a knee-high stump by the fireplace. Night after night she would crack walnuts to sell the walnut kernels. She had done it so long she was an expert. Nearly each time, she would have only four solid pieces from one walnut. When I tried to help, I would have six or seven pieces, most of them crushed. My sisters and I agreed we would not have had high school rings if it were not for brown hands and Mother's perfection in cracking walnuts.

I made my cash two ways. I was paid 15 cents a bushel for picking beans. I never made more than 45 cents per day. Our cousins owned Teagues' Cannery, and they had a route to pick up blackberries at various homes. We could not go out to pick until the dew dried off the berries, and the Teagues came by at 2:00 PM. I never got more than three gallons at 15 cents a gallon to make another 45 cents for the day. I put my change in a tin baking powder can so it would rattle loudly. I was really proud of that money. Since we could not have sheep and Mother could not card and spin wool thread and make our sweaters, I usually ordered a sweater from the Sears and Roebuck Catalogue with part of my beans and blackberry money.

No, I never worried about money, and we didn't have to work 9 to 5 either. Yes, I loved my life while living on the farm.

Tallulah Falls Railroad

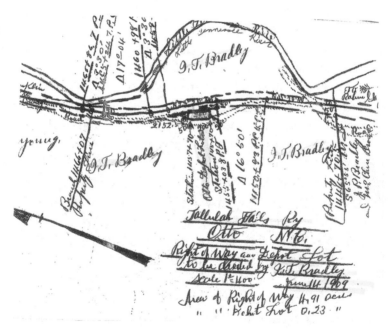

January 7, 1911, my daddy bought my grandparents' home and most of the land. The train tracks went through our farm. I always looked forward to the train's passing so I could wave to the passengers, engineers, and the conductors. I also waved to the two men, the Track Maintenance Inspectors, who rode the tracks on a handcar. This must have been hard work, as they had to pump with their feet on a wheel-like contraption to make it run while looking for defects on the tracks. Later these handcars had batteries and a motor so the men did not have to work so hard. Just think of the thousands and thousands of miles of railroads that had to be checked. If they found a defect, such as a bolt being loose, they had to get off the handcar and make repairs. These men were so friendly waving and hollering to us, I felt like I knew them. I wished they would come by every day.

We walked along the railroad tracks as much as we did the highway for we all knew the train's schedule. It was not only a passenger train; it was a freight train, also. It carried pulpwood and crossties, too, as outgoing freight.

I do know we rode the train a lot going to and from Franklin. I would tell Mother we needed to take our churn and milk for the train shook so much, butter would have been churned when we got home.

I have seen so much written about the Tallulah Falls Railroad that I know is not correct. For instance, I have a train schedule dated October 1, 1906, from Cornelia, Georgia, to Prentiss, NC, leaving Cornelia at 11:45 AM and arriving at Prentiss at 3:15 PM. The Railroad and Depot had to be constructed after July 31, 1909. A survey map dated June 14, 1909 shows I.T. Bradley, my grandfather, let Tallulah Falls Railroad have 4.91 acres for a right of way for the tracks and 0 .23 for the depot. The survey map and deed was recorded in the Macon County Court House July 31,1909. The Y turn around was in Franklin, not Prentiss. The train would have to go five miles north, through Grandpa's fields, to get to Prentiss for the Tallulah Railroad Company did not acquire the land until 1909. So much I have read is inaccurate.

Walt Disney made two movies on the Tallulah Falls Railroad. In 1951, "I'D CLIMB THE HIGHEST MOUNTAIN" opens in front of our home showing the Little Tennessee River and the train. Susan Hayworth was the star. In 1955, "THE GREAT LOCOMOTIVE CHASE" was filmed with Fess Parker as the star. There was talk that Walt Disney was going to make another film or buy the railroad for an excursion line. I believe the train stopped operating in 1955. However, I am not totally sure of this date. It was in receivership and, I suppose, not making any money. The railroad closed in 1961 with a $300,000.00 debt and went for scrap. Following is a postal card I bought when I was very young of the Otto Tallulah Falls Railroad train station. The opposite side of the depot had a waiting room for the passengers and the side you see on the card was for loading and unloading freight. I remember it very well.

CHAPTER TWENTY-TWO

Holidays On The Farm

Rambling Rose, above
Ivy bushes, top right
Wild Daisies, bottom

Decoration Day: In addition to all the work, there was a lot of pleasure involved in living in our small community. I can remember working with my daddy to get ready for decorating the graves at Asbury Church Cemetery. We would make several trips early Saturday morning from our farm to the cemetery with flowers; we called them ivy bushes, which were big balls of flowers. (They are now called laurel, I think. I still call them ivy.) We would gather armloads of wild daisies and the rambling roses, then decorate every grave after the men of the community had cleaned the graves. On Decoration Day, I always enjoyed listening to my elders reminiscing. While cleaning the graves, there were special tales being told that, as a child, gave me a special feeling of being part of the greater community. Other people were decorating in the same way.

Year round there were rough oak tables left out all around the church. After the graves were decorated, we children helped Mother carry loads of food to those tables as the other families were doing, too. It was better than a family reunion. It was a Community Reunion. All the people in the community knew to not miss it. People who had moved away would come back home for a visit just to participate in Decoration Day. There was so much hugging, laughing, and kissing while getting caught up on what had happened since the last Decoration Day.

For at least 25 years, I would dream I was a very small girl trying to reach up onto a table to get the last piece of meringue pie and some big man's hand would come down and get it while I was reaching for it. After eating, we went into the church for some announcements of deaths, births, and sicknesses, followed by speeches and a lot of old-time singing. With much disappointment, the day was over too soon.

The highway (now US 23 and US 441) was built, or upgraded, I believe, about the turn of the century. This was a major road project. A black worker died on the job and none of the churches would let him be buried in their cemetery. No one could find any of his family. Daddy let him be buried on our property at the edge of the woods so the grave wouldn't be plowed over. On Decoration weekend, Daddy always took flowers to his grave just like we did at Asbury Church. For a long time Daddy would say that no trees were growing on his grave. Years after my daddy died in 1947, my sister and I tried to find the grave. We did not.

I am sorry the date and name was changed in 1967 from Decoration Day to Memorial Day. The day was never the same after that.

The 4th of July: The Fourth of July brings back several memories, as that is when we got a store-bought bottle of drink and a big container of cinnamon buns. If you look forward to something for a long time, it is so good. Of course the drink was not cold, as the store didn't have electricity. But that drink was still special. Mother would save a long time to get this extra money for my parents, two sisters, and me to have these treats. Nowadays, we go to the refrigerator, get a drink, and never think how good it tastes. Probably half is wasted since we have no appreciation.

Mother would always try to have the first ears of corn and the first, fresh tomato for lunch on the Fourth of July. Now that was special. The ears of corn might not be fully developed, and the tomato might not be fully ripe; but those tastes were something else for us to look forward to.

In the afternoon, we would go up on our mountain and pick huckleberries (wild blueberries). I would always get covered with chiggers. Chiggers didn't get on my mother or sisters.

One year, everyone of all ages went up to Foy Dryman's mother's and aunt's homes at the head of Middle Creek (probably five or six miles from the church) to camp out in their pasture. This was just about as far as you could go on Middle Creek Road. It was known to have snakes. We were encouraged and repeatedly told, "Don't worry. We will keep a big bonfire all night, and they will not come near the fire." We enjoyed everything about the campout even the approximately 12 mile, round-trip walk to get there and go back to the church.

Christmas: I enjoyed our Christmas decorating. I am sure my daddy would have our Christmas tree picked out by July. In December, he would take us girls onto our mountain to hunt for a Christmas tree. We would go look at a dozen or more trees, but the first tree he would take us to would be the one we took home. At each tree after the first one, he would say, "Oh, this or that is wrong with this tree, it's not as pretty as that first one." We thought we were making the decision, but now I realize he had found the right tree months before we started looking.

We made all our decorations, such as mixing flour and water and dipping sycamore balls and hanging them on the tree. I never heard of electric Christmas tree lights for no one had electricity. We would cut little pieces of paper and make a paste with flour and water and paste them into a circle for a chain. We would pop popcorn to string on a thread for another chain. I still make the paper and popcorn chains. The family making and decorating our tree was something to remember. All the family time we spent together making our decorations made our tree very personal.

CHAPTER TWENTY-THREE

Other Entertainment

Most of our entertainment was from self-made things, using our imagination and the enjoyment of being with family and friends. I don't remember having a store-bought toy except a doll.

I had five girl friends that lived in about a two-mile radius. We were not more than two years apart in age. Our parents would let us walk from friend to friend's house, and we often spent the night with each other. We spent most of the time in each other's playhouses made up in our imaginations. We would lay sticks on the ground for the walls and room partitions. We used rocks for pretend furniture. One girl had an old abandoned building we used as a playhouse. My favorite play "house" was in the woods above the spring. In cold weather, our daddy let us use one corner of the barn loft to play in.

We played a lot of games such as, jump rope, hop scotch, marbles using little stones from the branch, tag, Simon Says, and many more. We always found something to do, and we never got bored.

With the family, I remember most playing checkers. We had a nail keg, which we also used as a seat, and a homemade checkerboard. We used different colored corn for the checkers. I liked playing with all my family except one sister. Every time she knew she was losing, her knee would accidently hit the board, and there would be corn all over the floor. I had to play with her because we took turns.

I remember having some good laughs with ridiculing our family singing. None of us could carry a tune. We would take a metal pie pan and hit it with our elbow and the side of our hand to try to make music. Since we knew the words, we would always sing, "Will The Circle Be Unbroken".

Visiting my grandparents who lived at Hickory Knoll community, about five miles from our home in Otto, we had a choice – we could either walk or ride in the wagon with my father. I walked. We walked on the railroad tracks for about half of the way. We knew everyone along the way, so we got to talk and laugh a lot since we visited folks as we walked. Going the five miles back home the same day didn't seem so far when we were young. A lot of the large family of 11 surviving children, and 70 grandchildren, came for Grandfather's birthday on the weekend closest to March 30. We had a jolly, good time then.

The first movie I saw was "Heidi" in the late 1930's. Mr. Will Corbin took his daughter, Margaret, and me to see it. Whoa!! The second movie in the late 1930's was "Gone With The Wind". I thought the Bradley family had some ownership in it for we had the book that my sister, Hazel, was awarded. Hazel won a county essay contest given by the U.D.C. when she was a senior at Franklin High School, Franklin, North Carolina. I was proud but didn't understand. Her teacher was Mrs. Helen Macon. I always thought Hazel was the smartest person in the world in so many things.

I also enjoyed activities planned by our church and the community. Our parents never let us go to public dances where I understand there was drinking and rough crowds. They never let us play cards, either.

I enjoyed going by myself up on the hill where I could have a 360-degree view of the sky. I didn't go unless it was a day with big, fluffy white clouds and a beautiful blue sky. I have never seen that color of blue reproduced on this earth. I wanted to get up in the clouds and lay down. I wondered where the clouds would be stored over night. When it rained, I wondered how the clouds could change size and colors to dark gray and black. I wondered where all the rain came from. I would find different animal shapes in the clouds. I had to look fast because they were constantly changing. My curiosity went wild. I didn't know it until I was an adult, but I was exercising my brain. I can't explain my joy the first time I had an airplane flight and could look down on the clouds. I was a child again.

I enjoyed the sounds around our farm: the roosters crowing early in the morning telling us it was time to start a new day, hens cackling when they laid an egg, church bells, cowbells, and birds singing, Whip-poor-wills and Hoot Owls in the evenings. It is not the same today as I am not making up what they are saying to each other and wondering how they learned to talk and sing. Today I miss all that and my mother calling me to lunch and the Tallulah Falls Railroad engine and whistle.

Part of our entertainment was enjoying riddles like I asked in a previous chapter. I have been telling this riddle for many, many years, and no one ever says, "Light the match first".

Presented to -

Hazel Bradley
by the U.D.C. as an Essay Prize
"war Reminiscences of my Community"

1939

*Mrs. Helen Mason -
teacher*

GONE
WITH THE
WIND

by
MARGARET MITCHELL

NEW YORK
THE MACMILLAN COMPANY
1936

CHAPTER TWENTY-FOUR

Cherokee Indians

On the east side, our farm was bordered by the Little Tennessee River. Along the bank of the river were lots of river canes. We needed to have them cut so they would not spread further into our land. The Indians made baskets and other items from the bark of the canes to sell in Cherokee. They needed the canes. These baskets were "the real thing" before most of what they sold came from China.

At least twice a year, I really looked forward to the Cherokee Indians coming to our farm to cut the canes since they brought us one or two papoose to play with.

The Indians spent hours cutting and trimming the canes, so we got to play with the babies for a long time. The babies would be in a cradleboard, which was used in the first few months of an infant's life when a portable carrier was necessary for the infant. I believe there was competition among the parents to see who could make the most decorated cradleboard. Each one was decorated so differently. All of them had a firm board for the frame, good padding, a footrest at the bottom, and a rounded cover over the baby's head for a shade and also a place for ornaments and sacred items for amusement. While walking or standing, the mother would strap this to her back. My sisters and I got to take the babies out of the cradleboards and hold them. They did not have to bring the babies; however, they did it so we could enjoy playing with them. This was a great pleasure and something to look forward to.

They also brought us one or two beautiful baskets made from our cane. We used the baskets at the barn, garden, and chicken house, not appreciating the value of these gifts. Mother did save one basket for herself and gave me one when I was very young. I kept my basket as a prize possession, moving it from town to town and house to house until I let The Museum of Appalachia at Norris, Tennessee, have it. If you have visited this museum, you may have seen it in The Hall of Fame Building with an article about me with a picture of the farm and the river canes. In the same building, you will see my name and articles three times. People from all over the world visit this museum. John Rice Irwin, the founder and a real good friend of mine, spent most of his life collecting over 250,000 items for the Museum. You should visit there if you have not already.

CHAPTER TWENTY-FIVE

Quilting

Quilting time was a party time, with friends meeting, eating, and enjoying themselves while they quilted. They made quilts for each other or someone else in need of a good, warm quilt. As a child, it seemed the quilters met at our home more than anywhere else. Our house was on the main highway and all local roads lead to our house.

Year round we kept the frames, when they were not in use, pulled up in two places to our ceiling. One was in our hall. Most homes had wide halls between the bedrooms on one side and the living room, dining room and kitchen on the other side. Usually the halls were opened to the direction the breeze would enter the home. Ours opened from the West to the East. This let fresh air into the other rooms. Sure felt good! We did not know what a fan was as we didn't have electricity. The other quilting frame was in the living room. We seldom used that room except when special company came in the cold weather. We usually entertained on the front porch. In the living room, we had a fireplace so the women were warm while quilting.

My sister, Hazel Bradley, wrote the following notes in 1955. She was the smartest person I have ever known. Hazel was visiting from her work as manager of the Classified Ads for the Cleveland Banner, Cleveland, Tennessee. Although I have been writing about things from my birth through my teenage years, this is an example of what happened all my life. So I will borrow Hazel's note. Aunt Octa, (not really my aunt but we called all people older than 50 Aunt or Uncle) had great back problems and walked bent over. Every time Aunt Octa got up to walk, three-year-old Sally would walk behind her all bent over, mocking her. I remember being told about Sally getting a spanking that day.

Ref: Granny Brown, Mamie Fulcher

A Quiltin' for Sally

Mrs. Emma Stiles; Mrs. Brown, Friend: Mrs. Wilson; Aunt Octa Bates

Bessie Bradley and Rose Stiles decided that while Sally had two great grandmothers living to have a "quiltin'" so that Sally, then about three, would have a keepsake with stitches by her mother, Rose Stiles, foster grandmother Bessie Bradley, and two great grandmothers, Emma Stiles and Mamie Brown.

On the appointed day, with the quilt in the frames in the front room at Bradley's, Rose brought the guests, the honored great grandmas, a neighbor, up the highway about two miles. Then Aunt Octa Bates arrived.

One of Mrs. Bradley's daughters, Hazel, was home for a visit. She wasn't quilting because the guests looked askance at each other's stitches and didn't welcome any amateurs. Then the amateurs were a trifle afraid of putting any stitches that would be subject to the scrutiny of those pros who had made many quilts for family covers, for gifts and in the case of Aunt Octa, to be sold by retirees in Ohio.

CHAPTER TWENTY-SIX

Worries

Above: The mountain front and center was our mountain. Behind that, the land was obtained by The Coweeta Experimental Forest by 1934.

I had three worries about the Government that my parents couldn't solve. Land was being taken, or bought for less than its value, for the establishment of several government projects. I was afraid we would have to move and there would be nothing my mother and daddy could do to prevent the move. I loved our land from the top of the mountain (official name "Little Mountain") through the fields and pastures to the bottomland bounded by the Little Tennessee River. I also enjoyed what is now known as US Hwy 23-441 and the Tallulah Falls Railroad, which ran parallel to the highway and through our property.

1: The Coweeta Experimental Forest was established in 1934 on nearly 4000 acres of land starting four miles from our home and nearer to the backside of our mountain. This was renamed Coweeta Hydrologic Laboratory in 1948. Now they have even more acreage. According to the Forest Service, this area has proven to be the source of some of the most influential research on forested watershed done in the world. The Civilian Conservation Corps workers (CCC young men) built roads, buildings, testing stations, and other permanent installations on the site during the 1930's.

2: Also in 1934, land was being acquired from counties adjoining Macon County, North Carolina, for The Great Smoky Mountains National Park, which opened June 15, 1934. My worry was: the government would come and take our place next. My parents would tell me no land was being taken in Macon County. The government took 521,896 acres; that is 800 square miles, of farmland, homes, churches, barns, and schools that were started by settlers in the late 1700's. Families, church members, relatives, schoolmates, and neighborhoods were separated and had to find new homes miles and miles apart.

The park has preserved some home places, churches, cabins, farmhouses, and barns for the tourists to see. I also like to go to Cataloochee, NC, in the fall and see the elk come out around the original church, school, and a farmhouse that were preserved. Although I am glad the visitor can enjoy these old home places, I try to not think about the citizens who had to make such a sacrifice to leave everything and hunt for a new place to live and work. I could not imagine leaving any of the above. I loved them all.

3: In the early 1930's, it really worried me when I started hearing about the Tennessee Valley Authority (TVA). In 1933, the TVA, a federally owned corporation created by a Congressional charter to provide navigation, flood control, electricity, fertilizer, and economic development was organized. I didn't know what electricity was, for we didn't have electricity until the summer of 1940. However, I heard farmers talking about the government saying "farmers are destroying their land and ruining their forests; and they (the Tennessee Valley Authority) were going to set things right."

In the 1920's and 1930's, Muscle Shoals, Alabama, was the first TVA core part of the New Deal's TVA where electricity was generated and fertilizer was produced. TVA said, "This would help the poor farmers' land they were destroying." Farmers loved their land. They knew better how to take care of it than the government. I would sit on our front porch and listen to every word these wise farmers had to say. They told me not to worry about our farm being taken. It didn't help but very little.

I have read that 94 percent of utility companies were privately owned in the early 1920's, mostly unregulated. That gave rise to the Public Utility Holding Company act in 1935, which lead to many private utility companies being bought by the federal government and others closed, for they could not compete with TVA.

TVA now services Tennessee, portions of Alabama, Mississippi, Kentucky and a little of both Georgia and Virginia. For Norris Lake, the first to be completed, I believe 2899 families were displaced. That amounts to about 13,000 people, and 5,226 graves were moved by 1936 when it was completed. We did not have to move off our beautiful farmland, for which I am grateful. TVA claims they have conveyed approximately 485,420 acres of property for recreation and preservation such as public parks, public access area, boating, fishing, swimming, camping sites, roadside parks, and wildlife refuges. I AM GLAD THIS IS NOT PART OF OUR FARM. However, my worries were real at the time.

I would like to write more about TVA as I live near their Headquarters in Knoxville, Tennessee, and live three miles from the beautiful Douglas Lake. However, this is supposed to be about my life through my teenage years, April 4, 1926 thru April 3, 1945.

CHAPTER TWENTY-SEVEN

1940's Brought Change

When I was a young girl, I could look from our farm, far and wide, and see four family farms. They were the Mozely's, Parrish's, Corbin's and ours. All bordered the Little Tennessee River. We all took pride in and loved our farms.

Tourists were coming to the mountains and probably did not understand family farming. They would stop by and tell my daddy, "Mr. Bradley, I want to buy a half acre right here with a view, privacy, a stream of water, and a garden spot."

They could not understand what it would have meant to cut out a half acre in the middle of our land. It was an insult, and it would be equal to someone walking into a store and telling the owner, "I want to buy this counter and your cash register." It would have been an insult to mess up their business.

I remember the first woman in our community to buy a car. She was a schoolteacher, and she was assigned a school on the opposite end of the county from her home. Her car was a maroon-colored Plymouth with a little back seat and the back window went straight down and the trunk went straight down. I was sorry for her when the color started fading.

I was a teenager until 1945. The 1940s were a completely, positively different time from the 1920's and 1930's. It would take 100 pages to write the difference. People began to get electricity and cars. After Pearl Harbor, the men were going into service and leaving home. The women were leaving to work in war plants never to return to their communities. This was the end of so many ways of life we had known. Families were separated, family farms were going out of existence, and little sawmills were going out of existence for the young men did not return home to work after the war. Young women wanted to continue to work and make money. Yes, every way of life was changing. I am so glad I was raised in the 20's and 30's. I went away to Western Union School in 1943 never to return to the farm, so I am not criticizing anyone else.

There are probably more out-of-state residents now living in Otto than the original families. I am thankful for them. When my mother was in the nursing home for over ten years and didn't speak to us during that time, we had to sell her property to pay the nursing home bills. We were so happy to say, "Welcome to our farm," to local and out-of-town people.

Before my daddy died in 1947, he was so pleased to have Asbury Methodist Church and Otto School on our property. He had not sold land for a house in the middle of his fields. I am also pleased that he didn't see all the original Otto buildings torn down. This included the first building in Otto that he and his family built and was the last to be torn down.

Asbury Methodist Church Built 1940

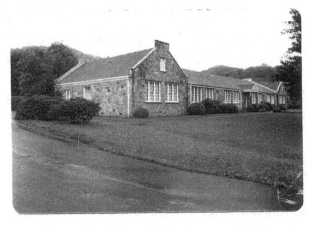

Otto Consolidated School. Across the drive from Asbury Methodist Church. Built 1940

Now we have lots of houses and the Otto Community Development Organization and Fire Hall buildings on the property. I am proud Ed R. and Bessie Rogers Bradley's family had a part in the development of Otto.

CHAPTER TWENTY-EIGHT

Leaving The Farm - Practical Education

I was 17 years old April 4th, 1943, and graduated from High School April 20th 1943. I knew my parents did not have the money to send me to college. If they had had the money, I would not have taken it. I planned to work a few years and then pay my way through college. I did not know many people who went to college except my teachers, and I was not going to be a teacher. My sister, Hazel, graduated from Brevard College. She got a great scholarship through The Farmer's Federation Company. My sister, Josephine, had always wanted to be a beautician. She went to beautician school, and my parents helped her get her own business, Jo's Beauty Shop, in Franklin, North Carolina. I remember I worked some for her. One of my jobs was to take a large jug of water and cut a long bar of soap into little pieces to make shampoo. You could not buy prepared shampoo.

World War II was going on, and a lot of people left the farming life for jobs or for military service. There was no way for me to make money on the farm. My daddy read or heard about an application for Western Union School. When he told me about it, I said, "What is Western Union?" We went to the pay telephone, one of just two telephones available in the community, and made a call to get more information. Since Daddy didn't have a car, he hired a driver to take me over the mountain to a town where I filled out the application. I was accepted for the training.

I left home on the bus on April 29th, 1943, (just nine days after graduating) for Western Union School in Gainesville, Georgia. The school was for students from nine states. I started my class May 3, 1943, and finished June 26th, 1943. I got on the bus again to go to my first assignment. For the next two months, I worked in three different offices, filling in for when an employee was on vacation or out sick.

After two and a half months of work, the manager of the Hendersonville office said, "Lotus, there is an opening for a Manager of Western Union in Tryon, North Carolina. I told them you would be good at it." I said, "Where is Tryon? They wouldn't have me because of my age and lack of experience." He said, "The job is yours if you will just say yes." He told me to ask for $1.00 more per day, as Tryon was a high-priced tourist town. I was making 32 cents an hour at that time. I had been in Hendersonville from August 7, 1943, until September 12, 1943. He had known me for about a month, and he knew what I was capable of doing. I didn't even know what would be expected of me. He sounded so sure I could do it, I said " yes." Of course, today I would say, "Because of the war, they couldn't get anyone else, so they hired me."

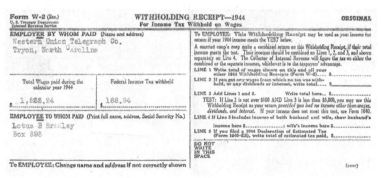

There I went on the bus again. Things were moving fast for someone 17 years and 5 months old. They had already arranged a room for me in a boarding house. In those days, women did not rent apartments; they lived in boarding houses. I doubt if there were apartments back then.

The first three or four weeks I was there, I was the most popular person in the county. I believe every person who had a son in the service came in to see me. In case the Government sent them one of those "Sorry to inform you that your son is missing in action, wounded in action, or killed," I would know them, where they lived, and who to (or not to) deliver messages. Outside the city, very few roads had names, and there were certainly no house numbers. All directions were from the main road using landmarks such as barns, color of houses, or kind of fences, etc. I did not know any of the roads or locations. All I knew was that I came in on a very crooked road from Hendersonville, North Carolina, to Tryon, North Carolina; so I had to keep a good log and have a good memory.

Western Union had a contract with the best taxi driver, Mr. Bishop, to deliver the messages. He could stay up to an hour if the family needed help in getting a doctor, getting relatives to the house, or other assistance. If he needed to stay longer, he had to call me.

I had sharp pains between my back ribs for at least 25 years when I thought of the following: A Mr. Durham came in to see me, I believe every time he came to town to remind me of his two sons; and, if I got a message, not to deliver it to his wife as she had heart problems. He wanted me to send any message to his daughter. One day he came in and said, "Well, I now have three boys over there." His 18-year-old son had joined one of the branches of service and was quickly sent overseas.

I felt like he knew he was going to get one of those messages. He was also concerned about Mrs. Durham. I think the message "your son is missing in action" was the worst. They didn't know if a son was dead, wounded and not getting treatment, or if they would ever know what happened to their son.

When I opened the Teletype in the mornings, usually the Government telegrams were first. One morning, the first message was to Mr. Durham, RFD # 2, Tryon, North Carolina.

I certainly knew him. He had been expecting this for months. The third telegram was to Mrs. Durham, Tryon, NC. (No RFD #). I had never heard Mr. Durham's wife's first name. The telegrams usually came in the father's name.

The Government required me to start delivering messages within an hour. I had Mr. Bishop on stand-by to take the first message out to Mr. Durham's daughter. Thank goodness emergency thinking kicked in. I would go to the Selective Service Office to find this young man's parents. The office wasn't due to open until my hour was up but an employee came in a little early. When I found out this was the Mr. Durham I knew and his wife, and knowing Mrs. Durham's heart condition, my next decision to make was whether to call Washington and get an extension of sending one or should Mr. Bishop take both messages at the same time. I decided to send both messages together. The family was glad I made that decision.

Here are a just few of the good memories:

The Tryon area had so many year-round, well-known residents and a lot of seasonal visitors who owned homes, or stayed at the many inns and the Oak Hall Hotel. A lot of these people were famous authors, artists, horse owners, or retired business people. They had visitors from all over the world. I learned so much from them every day by taking care of their telegrams. I cannot express how good they were to me.

Mrs. Calvin Coolidge spent, I believe, ten winters with the Dodge Motor Company family on top of White Oak Mountain five miles away from a telephone. She was so sweet and kind.

James Kimberly, Sr., retired president of Kimberly Clark Corp., and other family members, had homes in Tryon and Neenah, Wisconsin. He would come into the Western Union office and spend at least a half hour with me. He wanted me to tell him about being raised on a farm in the mountains of Western North Carolina during the 1920's and 1930's. He told me we had a Family Enterprise, with each one having their jobs and doing them. This didn't mean much to me until I was older and I realized how true it was.

Another famous person, Charles A. Beard, a great American historian, was spending his winter at Pinecrest Inn in Tryon while Life Magazine was featuring him in several issues with part of his new book, "The Republic". He would walk about one mile to the Western Union office and spend time with me, just like James Kimberly, Sr., to talk about my living on the farm. He brought me the January 17, 1944, autographed copy of Life Magazine with his picture and stories about him. I appreciated such a famous man walking two miles round trip to bring me the Life Magazine, but today I appreciate it even more.

Lady Nancy Astor, the first woman in the English Parliament, came to Tryon to visit her sister, Nora Flynn, wife of Lefty Flynn. In my spare time, I was the local reporter to the Asheville Citizen Times. When they heard Lady Astor was coming to town, they ask me to get an interview with her. I told them they needed to get a special reporter to come and interview such an important person.

I called Mrs. Flynn and told her about my conversation with the editor of the paper. She said, "Don't bring anyone else. You and I will interview her. You bring the pencil and paper, and I will ask her the questions. You write the questions and answers down." I had been in her home before, and I knew we would go to the long dining room table where they entertained so many famous people. Lady Astor sat at the end of the table, and Mrs. Flynn and I sat at the end of long benches on each side of the table. Lady Astor and Mrs. Flynn were two of the famous Langhorne sisters of Virginia. We had a good time laughing and talking. Lady Astor and her husband, Waldorf, lived in a castle in England with lots of servants. That night, Lady Astor spoke to the public at the high school. She kept all of us laughing. You would not have known she was such a famous person. Please look her up on the Internet. Mr. and Mrs. Flynn were so good to me. I wish

I had kept a list of gifts they brought me from all over the world.

I was so comfortable talking to anyone, as I was always myself due to the way I was raised, speaking the Queen's English, and remembering how my parents taught me to be proud. I also remembered what Mrs. Green, my teacher, wrote in my autograph book: "Be what you is, and not what you ain't; because if you is what you ain't, then you ain't what you is," by Hambone. I was always myself and felt comfortable.

I had to ride the bus approximately 100 miles to go home to see my parents on the farm. Supervisors of Western Union would tell me I could go on vacation on a certain day. Then a few days before I was supposed to go home, they would advise me that they could not find a substitute for me. My heart was broken as well as my parents were disappointed. This happened several times.

Mr. Carson, a Lumber Wholesaler or Lumber Broker, had been trying to get me to come to work with him. He was out of town a lot, and I worried over his telegrams when I couldn't deliver them. I felt like I knew a lot about his business. A few weeks before my 19th birthday I said, "Yes, I want to work with you." I am so glad I did. The business was ever changing. At first, most all lumber went to companies making war products, and then houses were being built. Yes, it was ever changing after the war when life was getting back to normal.

I loved calling lumbermen from coast to coast and Canada, talking with them the first time, getting their confidence, and continuing to do business with them for years and years. I am glad I learned at an early age to have confidence in myself by just being myself. I described myself as a North Carolina Mountain Hillbilly.

The lumber manufacturers and the buyers were also surprised that I was a female in their male-dominated business. I was the only female in this business. I was a Lumber

Wholesaler for 35 years and would still be doing it if it were not for the recession while Jimmy Carter was President. During that time, there were interest rates of 20%, inflation was 20%; and businesses were dropping like flies. There was very little business, and I was afraid to sell to the former best-paying customers because they could go broke overnight, especially when so many of their customers were going broke. I had to say goodbye to a business I loved.

I am sure I learned more the first year of work when I was 17 than I would have in a full, four-year degree in college. This is mostly due to the people I came in contact with, my former teaching by my parents, my church, and my work ethic on the farm. It would take a thousand pages to write about my memories during my 17th, 18th and 19th years. I learned on the farm to take the good and bad. That is life.

LIFE'S COVER: Charles A. Beard has profile of a Roman senator and the well-stocked mind of a classical philosopher. Here this great American historian sits looking over the Blue Ridge mountains of North Carolina and ponders the destiny of the country he knows so well. Beard's knowledge and faith are eloquently expressed in his new book *The Republic*, parts of which are being published in this week's LIFE and in future issues (*see p. 47*).

ABOUT THE AUTHOR

Throughout this book, you have witnessed the values Lotus Bradley Plott learned from living on her family's farm, and by being part of a loving family, church, and community. She has carried those same values into her varied careers, first as a caring Manager of a Western Union office, then being a coast to coast, United States and Canada, Lumber Broker in a male-dominated business, and lastly, a caring realtor. During her real estate era was when I experienced, first hand, how she emulated one of those Mother Hens she describes in this book. She went above and beyond what most realtors do. She led us to a proper nesting site and became a good friend in the process. I felt more as an adopted child than a client.

Lotus was married twice, and has one son, Roger Stephen Plott, who resides in the Pacific Northwest. She has been a widow since February 1981. Her many friends in her current community, church, and former business associates keep her busy and involved. There is no "retirement" even though she is now in her 90's.

To know Lotus is to love her. I hope you enjoyed reading all the gems of wisdom she has shared either by her public speaking engagements or in this book she has lovingly produced. To quote her, "She is what she is, not what she ain't."

I have been pleased and proud to be part of this project of saving some of her educational and inspirational information.

Kay Black, friend

CPSIA information can be obtained
at www.ICGtesting.com
Printed in the USA
BVHW091343251021
619802BV00011B/303